Succeeding
WITH English
Language
Learners

Succeeding
with English
Language
Learners

A GUIDE FOR
BEGINNING TEACHERS

THOMAS S. C. FARRELL

CORWIN PRESS
A SAGE Publications Company
Thousand Oaks, California

KH

For information:

Corwin Press
A Sage Publications Company
2455 Teller Road
Thousand Oaks, California 91320
www.corwinpress.com

Sage Publications Ltd.
1 Oliver's Yard
55 City Road
London EC1Y 1SP
United Kingdom

Sage Publications India Pvt. Ltd.
B-42, Panchsheel Enclave
Post Box 4109
New Delhi 110 017 India

Printed in the United States of America

Library of Congress Cataloging-in-Publication Data

Farrell, Thomas S. C. (Thomas Sylvester Charles)
Succeeding with English language learners: A guide for beginning
teachers/Thomas S. C. Farrell.
    p. cm.
Includes bibliographical references (p.) and index.
ISBN 1–4129–2438–3 (cloth: acid-free paper) — ISBN 1–4129–2439–1
(pbk.: acid-free paper) 1. English language—Study and teaching—Foreign
   speakers—Handbooks, manuals, etc. I. Title.
PE1404.F359 2006
428.′0071—dc22   2005015863

This book is printed on acid-free paper.

05   06   07   08   09   10   9   8   7   6   5   4   3   2   1

Acquisitions Editor:	Faye Zucker
Editorial Assistant:	Gem Rabanera
Production Editor:	Beth A. Bernstein
Copy Editor:	Brenda Weight
Typesetter:	C&M Digitals (P) Ltd.
Proofreader:	Andrea Martin
Indexer:	Teri Greenberg
Cover Designer:	Rose Storey

1/28/08

Contents

Preface

It has now been long established in general education research that learning to teach is a complex process and the first years of teaching have an important impact on the future careers of beginning teachers. Studies on teacher socialization all agree on one issue: beginning teachers need assistance in the form of support during their first years of teaching. The primary purpose of *Succeeding With English Language Learners: A Guide for Beginning Teachers* is to provide crucial support for English language teachers at all levels in their first years to help make the transition from the teacher education institution to the real classroom smoother.

Another purpose for this book is that sometimes teachers of other content areas are either (a) asked to teach English as a second language (ESL) as an extra subject without proper training or certification in teaching ESL or (b) getting more ESL students in their content subject classes and do not know how to teach these students. This book, especially Chapters 3 through 9, will give them many strategies for teaching each English language skill area as well as for assessing the progress of their students in English. Thus they will be better placed to serve their less-language-proficient students and be better able to make decisions about whether their students need ESL placement or can be moved into mainstream content classrooms after a period of ESL lessons.

Many books on language teaching present a range of concepts, theories, methods, and techniques without giving readers any specific methods or strategies of language teaching that will get them through their first years as a teacher. In contrast, *Succeeding With English Language Learners: A Guide for Beginning Teachers* provides practical strategies and examples and also gives beginning teachers insight into what they can expect during their first years as language teachers, inside and outside the classroom. The book is grounded in theory, yet it is written for new teachers in accessible language and provides strategies they can implement immediately by engaging in the exploratory breaks. Later they can read the theory that supports the strategies they implement in their classes, as each strategy is explained and referenced. In other words, the book is user friendly for new teachers.

The main thesis of *Succeeding With English Language Learners: A Guide for Beginning Teachers* is that a strategic approach to teaching speaking, grammar, writing, and reading to all these students can help them better cope. Additionally, teachers in their first years can find easy-to-use techniques that they can put into action immediately and, if they are interested (and have time), they can look up the list of references so they can further develop this strategic approach to their teaching.

Each chapter in *Succeeding With English Language Learners: A Guide for Beginning Teachers* is clearly structured to help language teachers in their first years navigate clearly through the text. The first chapter provides a case study of one language teacher as a backdrop to the important issues of stages of development and support that many first-year language teachers typically face. They also learn what to expect from colleagues, the school, and the community.

Additional chapters provide first-year teachers with ideas on lesson planning (Chapter 2), classroom management (Chapter 3), and specific strategies and approaches to teaching all the skill areas (reading, writing, grammar, speaking, and listening). This is not overly theoretical and offers first-year teachers specific teaching strategies they can easily implement to teach each skill area that will get them through their first years. The theory behind the method is provided. Each of the chapters on teaching the skill areas is clearly outlined, from an introduction, to an explanation of the skill, to guidelines for preparing lesson plans to teach that skill, to, finally, providing at least one tried-and-tested strategic approach to teaching that skill. In addition, Chapter 9 discusses language assessment and outlines various ways language teachers can test oral and written language. The final chapter of the book, "Professional Development," deals with the future development of teachers in their first years by offering them the tools to become reflective practitioners.

Although *Succeeding With English Language Learners: A Guide for Beginning Teachers* is suitable for both preservice and second and foreign language teachers in their first years of teaching, it is also suitable for ESL and English as a foreign language (EFL) teachers in the primary and secondary grades who need a refreshing look at what they do. This audience can include teachers who are teaching in ESL pull-out programs or even in subject-area "immersion" classrooms that include native English speakers in addition to ESL learners. Although many of the examples used in each chapter are from both ESL and EFL settings, teachers of any second or foreign language will benefit from reading this book. The book can be used as a text in both undergraduate and graduate education, language, and/or linguistics courses (language arts, MED, MA, TESOL, etc.). This book can be used by nonnative and native speakers of English.

I have outlined strategic approaches to teaching all the skill areas in each chapter. It should be noted, however, that these activities should be taken only as suggestions and not as prescriptions. Teachers are invited to adapt and create their own exercises after each strategy has been explained. These strategic approaches are equally applicable to teachers of very young learners, teachers of teens, and teachers of adults. In many cases, all teachers must do is make small and simple modifications to the strategic approach that is presented so that it suits a particular group of students. This is the main reason why these strategic approaches are included in this book. I hope you enjoy *Succeeding With English Language Learners*.

—Thomas S. C. Farrell

ACKNOWLEDGMENTS

I would like to thank Faye Zucker at Corwin Press for all her encouragement and also my wife, Mija, and my daughters, Sarah and Ann Farrell, for their continued patience with me as I develop these books.

Corwin Press gratefully acknowledges the contributions of the following reviewers:

Elise Geither
Instructor
Baldwin-Wallace College
Berea, OH

Joanne E. Ho
English Department Chair
Clark High School
Las Vegas, NV

Theresa Rouse
Superintendent/Principal
San Lucas Union School District
San Lucas, CA

Verena Shanin
ESOL Teacher
Berea Middle School
Greenville, SC

About the Author

 **Thomas S. C. Farrell** is an associate professor in applied linguistics at Brock University, Canada. He has been involved with ESL and applied linguistics for the past 27 years and has written extensively on topics such as reflective practice, language teacher development, and language teacher education. His recent books include *Reflective Practice in Action* (2004, Corwin Press), *Reflecting on Classroom Communication in Asia* (2004, Longman), and *Professional Development for Language Teachers* (2005, Cambridge University Press, coauthored with Jack Richards).

CHAPTER ONE

Teaching in the First Year

Finally, you have made it to a "real" classroom. You may have received a shock, though, because it is different than you had expected, and your teacher education courses may not have prepared you as fully as you would have hoped for this new environment; you are now faced with new students, new colleagues, and new administrators, and you may feel bewildered about what to do. You must now realize that, from this moment onward, your teaching career is totally up to you. You must decide how, when, and, sometimes, what you will teach. So the transition from the protected life in the teacher-training institution to life in a real school classroom (no matter at what level) is not an easy one for most new teachers, and it has often been characterized as a type of reality shock in which the ideals that were formed during teacher training are replaced (sometimes forcefully) by the reality of school life (Veenman, 1984). This being so, teachers in their first years are faced with many challenges that are not always easy to negotiate, and they have special needs and interests that are very different from their more experienced colleagues.

The purpose of this chapter is to outline and discuss some of the challenges English language teachers can experience as they are socialized through different stages of development during their first years as English language teachers and/or "immersion" language teachers, regardless of the context. In this chapter, I hope to raise your level of awareness of the possibility of these problems occurring as a first step to recognizing their origin and, hopefully, allowing for a smooth transition into the profession of English language teacher.

To help highlight some of the challenges that English language teachers face in their first years, when making the transition from the teacher education program to the first-year classroom, I make use of the scenario of a U.S. English language (ESL) teacher (Stacy) as she made this same transition. The scenario is built around a composite of several first-year teachers that I have researched in different contexts (ESL/EFL and language immersion contexts) in the past 10 years, and, as such, all the events that I report in this scenario are real and, I hope, instructive for future English language teachers. The scenario is meant to be used as a reflective device so that new teachers can really see their own situations and compare them with what is reported in this chapter.

Exploratory Break 1.1
Teaching in the First Years

- What support do you think you will need during your first years as an ESL/EFL teacher?
- Where do you think you can get this support?
- Do you think the school or institution will give this support? Why? Why not?
- Do you think individuals within the school or institution can support you?
- Who will you get to help you during your first years?
- How can they support you?
- Can you think of any other people or places you can go for support during your first years as a language teacher?

FIRST-YEAR DEVELOPMENT

Different scholars in the field of education have outlined different stages (some call it phases) that teachers go through in their first years. I present two models: the early and influential Fuller and Brown (1975) model of stages of development and the more recent, and more detailed, Maynard and Furlong (1995) model of the stages first-year teachers go through (there are many more models).

Fuller and Brown

Fuller and Brown (1975) talk about a developing sequence of concerns for new teachers. They describe two general stages of development for beginning teachers. The first stage is characterized by survival and mastery and the second stage presents an either/or dichotomy of development: either settling into a state of resistance to change or staying open to adaptation and change of their practice. In the early stage, there are concerns about survival. Teachers' idealized concerns (before entering the classroom) are replaced by concerns about their own survival as teachers.

They are also concerned about control of the class and the content of their instruction. In the later stage, teachers become concerned about their teaching performance, including the limitations and frustrations of the teaching situation. Much later, Fuller and Brown suggest, teachers become more concerned about their students' learning and the impact of their teaching on this learning.

Exploratory Break 1.2
Stages of Development in the First Years

Fuller and Brown (1975) suggest two main stages of development and, within each stage, a continuum of extremes as follows:

Stage I: From survival in the classroom to mastery of the classroom

Survival ————————————————————— Mastery

Stage II: From a state of resistance to change to staying open to adaptation

Resistance ————————————————————— Adaptation

- Where on the continuum are you placed within each stage?
- How do you know you are in that particular place?
- Describe as best you can your particular stage of development at this moment in your teaching career.

Maynard and Furlong

More recently, Maynard and Furlong (1995, pp. 12–13) have presented a more complex picture (than Fuller and Brown) of beginning teacher development and suggest that teachers go through five stages of development during their first years: early idealism, survival, recognizing difficulties, reaching a plateau, and moving on. These first-year teachers' stages of development are explained as follows.

Early Idealism. This first stage sees the beginning teacher strongly identifying with the students while rejecting the image of the older, cynical teacher. Many beginning teachers are gung ho about getting on with the job for which they were educated, that of teaching language. They tend to skirt staff-room politics, as "this is not the reason they became a teacher." They are fixated on their students' attempts to learn the language.

Survival. In the survival stage, beginning teachers react to the reality shock of the classroom environment and all that entails. They have just realized that teaching is not easy regardless of the amount of training and education they have received. Beginning teachers now feel a bit overwhelmed by the whole task of teaching; individual lessons become a blur and they cannot manage their classrooms as effectively as they thought possible in Stage I. They cannot follow the progress (or the lack) in each individual student as they had wanted to. In a kind of desperation, beginning teachers want to survive with quick-fix methods to get them through lessons. These quick-fix methods help and provide some respite from the constant demands of teaching.

Recognizing Difficulties. Awareness of the difficulties of teaching, the next stage of development, according to Maynard and Furlong (1995), is when beginning teachers gain more insight into the difficulties of teaching and the causes of these difficulties. They now begin to recognize that teachers are limited in terms of what they can achieve and what they can change in the system and/or their classrooms. They are focused on their performance as a teacher. Now the teacher enters a self-doubt stage and wonders if he or she can make it as a teacher.

Reaching a Plateau. Following the self-doubt stage is the next step, when beginning teachers find themselves better able to cope in different and sometimes difficult situations; they even meet with some success during this stage. They want to establish routines of teaching within their own classrooms. However, they also develop a resistance to trying new approaches and methods so as not to upset the newly developed routines. They are focused more on successful classroom management and not as much on student learning. Success is being achieved (in the beginning teachers' eyes), and they do not want to do anything to upset this status quo that has been so difficult to achieve.

Moving On. The last stage, moving on, is when new teachers begin to focus more on the quality of student learning and the beginning teacher really begins to develop. Maynard and Furlong (1995) suggest that the beginning teacher needs a lot of support at this stage or he or she will not be able to develop further as a result of possible burnout. Maynard and Furlong (pp. 12–13) suggest that if the teacher remains unsupported, "there is a danger of burnout by committed [new] teachers trying to cope alone, or the 'moving on' grinding to a halt."

Exploratory Break 1.3
Stages of Development

Maynard and Furlong (1995, pp. 12–13) outline the following five stages of development teachers go through in their first years:

Early idealism: New teacher identifies with students and rejects older, cynical teachers

Survival: New teacher reacts to reality shock/feels overwhelmed/seeks quick-fix methods

Recognizing difficulties: New teacher becomes more aware of complexity of teaching/realizes teachers *are* limited/enters stage of self-doubt—can I make it as a teacher?

Reaching a plateau: New teacher starts to cope with routines of teaching/develops a resistance to new approaches and methods

Moving on: New teacher begins to focus on quality of student learning

- Do you agree with Maynard and Furlong's stages of development for a first-year teacher? Why? Why not?
- Which stage of development best describes where you are at the moment?

Part of my reasons for mapping out these different stages of development is to raise your level of awareness of the idea of stages of development—that not all about teaching can be mastered in the first years, but that it is all right; do not be too hard on yourself in these first years. Awareness of these different stages (you may want to consider naming them with different vocabulary that best suits your personal experiences) may help you recognize what you are experiencing in your first years and realize that you are not alone and that these are common experiences of first-year teachers. This awareness may also help you move through the stages smoothly because you realize that you are developing normally as a teacher.

SCENARIO: STACY'S FIRST YEAR

Stacy had enrolled in a one-year teacher education program to certify her as a second language teacher. Stacy already had a BA (English language) degree. The students in this teaching English as a second language (TESOL) certificate program were in a 10-month program in which they were exposed to teaching practice and theory classes. On graduating, Stacy obtained a position teaching English as a second language in a U.S. high school. What follows is an account of the stages of development Stacy went through during her first year. Read about Stacy's development during her first year as a language teacher and see what similarities and differences you notice in comparison to your experiences.

STACY'S STAGES OF DEVELOPMENT

First Semester

Stacy seems to have gone through several stages during her first semester as a teacher. First, she entered the school with some early idealism characterized by a strong identification with the students, as she really wanted to make a difference in their lives. She really wanted her students, most of whom were recent immigrants to the United States, to succeed in learning English so that they could soon enter mainstream classes. Stacy began to reject many of the older, cynical teachers at the school as the first weeks went by.

Then, as she moved through her first semester as a teacher, she suffered a series of shocks because of the difference between what she had learned in her teacher certification course and the reality of the classroom. In her quest to survive this stage, Stacy sought quick fixes for the discipline problems she was experiencing with one of her classes, but even though these quick fixes seemed to work, she still encountered some difficulties with many of the classes and her communication with her colleagues was next to zero as, she said, they kept their distance.

Stacy next entered a more settled stage, when she slowly began to recognize these difficulties for what they were—their source, their causes, and their result, but she still wondered if she would make it as a teacher. She said that she was bewildered with all the reading and marking of the exam papers as well as all the other duties a teacher has: "I thought I was the 'misfit' in the department and the school." These reflections began toward the end of her first semester and the beginning of the second semester during her first year as a teacher.

Second Semester

During her second semester, Stacy began to cope better with her classes (her teaching methods and classroom management improved). She had established certain routines both inside and outside the classroom, and she was trying to fit into the culture of the school. As noted previously, Maynard and Furlong (1995) call this stage "reaching a plateau." After this, Stacy started to pay more attention to the quality of her students' learning; in other words, she was "moving on," Maynard and Furlong's (1995) final stage of development during a teacher's first year. Or was she? Actually, Stacy realized that she found herself moving back and forth between these stages rather than moving on, and her position usually depended on what she was required to do by the school. Nevertheless, toward the end of the first year, Stacy began to "see" finally why she had wanted to be a teacher in the first place as she started to focus on the quality of her students' learning. She said that she realized her real reason for being a teacher was to help her students become better users of English so they could enter the main-stream courses. She is now able to reflect on what has influenced this philosophy:

> I have a definite philosophy of teaching: I think that all students always come first. If anything will not benefit the students, I will scrap it or play it down.

Exploratory Break 1.4
Stacy's First Years of Development

- Do you think Stacy's experiences are typical for a first-year language teacher? Why? Why not?
- If you are a teacher during your first year or years, what stage do you think you are at now?
- Did you, or do you think you will, go through all the stages?
- If you are a first-year language teacher at this time, what stage do you think you are at in your development (based on Maynard and Furlong's stages)?
- What is your philosophy of teaching the English language—ESL, immersion, and so forth?

FIRST YEARS OF SUPPORT

It is quite evident from Stacy's story that when teachers leave their teacher education or training program and move to real teaching situations in institutions, either university-based language training centers, commercial language schools in an ESL or EFL setting, or regular school districts, they more often than not feel isolated because they rarely experience the collegial collaboration (Hargreaves, 1994) that was promoted in the training courses. In many language teacher education courses, teachers are asked to work in small groups to study various methods of instruction and other such tasks; however, when they move to a job, there may be little, if any, peer support.

Most studies on teacher socialization, both in the general education literature and in TESOL, agree on one issue: beginning teachers need support during their first year of teaching. Support may be crucial because beginning teachers have found their first year a period of great anxiety (Johnson, 1996; Veenman, 1984). This support, especially support in the skills of teaching and emotional support, can come from school authorities and from colleagues within the school (Odell & Ferraro, 1992). The contents of this book will give new teachers full support for the skills of teaching ESL and EFL; however, it seems that the single most influential factor in teacher socialization for beginning teachers is their relationships with their colleagues during their first years as teachers (Jordell, 1987).

During their first years, novice teachers have two main jobs: teaching and learning how to teach. During their first years, teachers have special needs and interests that are different from those of their more experienced colleagues (Calderhead, 1992). Calderhead remarked that for beginning teachers, the first year is a fast-paced period in which the novice learns how to adapt to the culture of the school, especially in terms of principles of behavior and common school ideals.

For example, at the level of the "school as workplace," one of the special needs first-year teachers should consider is the influence of teaching colleagues. This is important, for it may be the case that several different "teacher cultures" exist in one school and that novice teachers are faced with the dilemma of which one to join (Carew & Lightfoot, 1979).

STACY'S SUPPORT

Williams, Prestage, and Bedward (2001) suggest that the culture of any school in which a beginning teacher works exists on a continuum, from a highly individualistic school culture to a collaborative culture where all the teachers are willing to help one another. Stacy found herself in a school that exhibited a culture of individualism. Stacy, not being allowed to observe any colleagues' classes, manifested this culture of individualism in the school. This was not helped by situational constraints such as

Stacy's physical isolation from the main staff room, as she was placed in a separate office on the opposite side of the block. There were limited opportunities for sharing because colleagues were not easily visible or accessible since they were not all sharing the same staff room. Stacy's physical location denied her access to opportunities for support.

Lack of communication with her other colleagues was, in fact, the main dilemma Stacy said she faced during her first year: "I didn't talk much with the other teachers because they were always busy and into cliques . . . only two new teachers [from the same teacher-training institution] are here." Stacy continued to talk about the different types of teachers she noted at her school and the feeling that these "cliques" made it hard for her and the other new teachers to adjust during their first year. She explained the different types of teachers in the school:

> I see three types of teachers: the group that came together three years before [from the teacher-training institution] . . . I think there are two of them. The older teachers transferred from other schools all stick together. Also, we have the older teachers who have been here a long time and keep to themselves.

Although the teacher-training institute said that she would have a mentor, Stacy noted that after one introduction, she had no more communication with her "mentor." Stacy only met her mentor one time during her first year and this during her first week in the school. She said that she really worries about forming good professional relationships with her colleagues.

Exploratory Break 1.5
Stacy's First Years of Support

- Do you think Stacy's experiences with support (or the lack of it) are typical of a first-year language teacher? Why? Why not?
- What kind of assistance do you think you will need when you start teaching in a school or institution for the first time?
- Who will you ask for this assistance?
- Do you think the school or institution will provide this support for you?
- How can you prepare for this support before you go to the school or institution?

TEACHING IN THE FIRST YEAR: KEY PLAYERS

Teachers in their first years can help themselves by becoming aware of just which people and organizations are involved in their induction and socialization processes. I see two key players (there are more players, but it is best to focus on the main players) as having a crucial role to play for the successful induction of language teachers into the profession of teachers, and you may be surprised to see that you are one of them: the school that the teacher starts teaching in and the teacher himself or herself.

The School: A Mentor

Each school should appoint a trained mentor to help new teachers through their first years. Of course, this is mandated in many school districts, but that is just the problem—it is mandated but not taken seriously. Many times the mentor is not trained for the position and sees it as an imposition on his or her time, and apart from greeting the new teacher and showing him or her the staff room and how to work the photocopy machine, not much direction is given to new teachers about how to navigate the classroom or how to deal with new colleagues. For example, in Stacy's case, a properly trained mentor could have provided a more sheltered experience during her first semester and year, and she or he could have acted as a bridge between the new and the more established teachers at the school. Research has indicated that beginning teachers who are carefully mentored are more effective teachers in their early years, since they learn from guided practice rather than depending on trial-and-error efforts alone. Additionally, mentored novice teachers tend to leave the teaching profession at a rate lower than nonmentored novices.

TESOL is no different when it comes to mentorship; this may be especially true not only for new teachers but also for teachers new to ESL. For example, in many school districts, teachers are being asked to teach ESL students without any training, and they, too, need guidance about how to deal with these wonderful students from diverse cultures and backgrounds.

So, properly trained ESL mentors are also vital if new teachers are to be guided safely through their first years. Malderez and Bodoczky (1999, p. 4) describe five different roles these ESL mentors can play:

1. They can be models who inspire and demonstrate.

2. They can be acculturators who show mentees the ropes.

3. They can be sponsors who introduce the mentees to the "right people."

4. They can be supporters who are there to act as sounding boards, should mentees need to let off steam.

5. They can be educators who act as sounding boards for the articulation of ideas to help new teachers achieve professional learning objectives.

I think these five roles can be a wonderful blueprint for principals and teacher educators who are involved in setting up mentorship programs, and they are also good guidelines for new teachers about the role of a mentor. New teachers can go through this list and ask their mentors to fulfill these roles.

Exploratory Break 1.6
Mentors

- Have you had any experiences with a mentor during your first years as a language teacher? Describe these experiences.
- Can you think of any other roles a mentor of language teachers should play besides Malderez and Bodoczky's (1999) five roles?
- Which of Malderez and Bodoczky's five roles that mentors can play did your mentor exhibit?
- Did your mentor exhibit any other roles?

Teaching Hours

Teachers in their first year should have fewer teaching hours than their more experienced colleagues in order to give them time to adjust to the realities of the job. This sounds reasonable, but principals often see new teachers with lots of energy as a resource to be used to the maximum immediately because, many times, the school they are appointed to has been undersupplied with teachers. It could be that in some schools, new teachers' skills are taken for granted and thus they are given full responsibilities from the first day of work. Stacy made a sudden jump from 16 periods to 35 periods, which was a real shock for her. This "shock" could destabilize already-anxious new teachers and have adverse effects well beyond their first year of teaching. These teachers can end up in such stressed-out states that they abandon the profession after only a short period of time (Varah, Theune, & Parker, 1986). Not only did Stacy have this increased teaching load, but she also had other duties that included marking exam papers and getting involved in extracurricular activities after school hours with the students. It is interesting that the principal did not find this a problem and remarked that new teachers have to "learn how to work smart." Nevertheless, Stacy felt that sometimes she did not have time to understand what she was doing. So, special timetable arrangements (at least during the first semester) should be made for new teachers in order to give them time to adjust to school life. New teachers cannot do much about this, but you could try to make a case for why you need the extra time to adjust.

Exploratory Break 1.7
Teaching Load

- Do you think Stacy had too many teaching hours and classes during her first year as a teacher? Why? Why not?
- Do you think first-year teachers should have fewer hours than more experienced teachers? Why? Why not?
- How many hours do you think first-year teachers should be expected to teach each week?
- How many hours a week do you expect to teach during your first year as a teacher?
- How would you justify (to the school head or principal) teaching fewer hours during your first year on the job? What reasons or arguments would you present to the school head or principal to justify teaching fewer hours?
- What would you do during the time off?

Nature of Classes

Connected to the teaching load is the nature, or type, of classes a new teacher is assigned to teach. Stacy was given many lower-proficiency classes in English language to teach. This responsibility placed a heavy burden on Stacy, because she had to deal not only with her students' underachieving in English, but also with their behavioral problems. It may be that these extra problems for new teachers could overload their psychological adjustment to the school. "Difficult" classes should only be given to beginning teachers under the guidance of a mentor or avoided altogether during the first year (see Chapter 3 on classroom management for more discussion on discipline).

Exploratory Break 1.8
Nature of Classes During the First Years

- Do you think first-year teachers should be given higher-level (in terms of language proficiency) classes only? Why? Why not?
- Do you think first-year teachers should be asked to teach lower-level (in terms of language proficiency) classes only? Why? Why not?
- Do you think first-year teachers should be asked to teach all levels of classes? Why? Why not?

The New Teacher

The beginning teacher himself or herself plays a vital role (some may say the beginning teacher has more responsibility than the other major players) in recognizing the reality of life in a school and, as such, should remain open to advice from the school personnel (the principal, mentor, and senior teachers). Lortie (1975) has best characterized the relationships that Stacy seems to have experienced with her colleagues during her first year: "live and let live, and help when asked" (p. 195). An important question is, did Stacy ask for guidance or was she waiting to be told what to do? Stacy may have given up too early, or easily, on her senior colleagues since they may have been burdened with their own heavy teaching loads. It may have been wiser for Stacy to become more assertive and ask for advice and assistance from her senior colleagues rather than waiting for them to intervene.

For example, beginning teachers like Stacy could become more proactive by drawing up a list of questions about the school and requirements for beginning teachers before they enter the school. These questions may include (but are not limited to) the following:

School

What is the organization of the school? Do I have a copy of the staff handbook, school rules, and any other school brochures? Who are the nonteaching staff members (clerical, computer and science technicians, librarians, and photocopy helpers) that I can ask for assistance?

Organization

Whom do I report directly to? Does the school have an induction program for beginning or new teachers? Who is my mentor? How often should I meet my mentor? What are my duties during recess, lunch, and after school? Do I have extracurricular activities? Do I have to teach remedial classes? What is my timetable? Where are my classrooms?

Subject

What classes will I be teaching and is there a written syllabus for each class? What are the required textbooks? What are the schemes of work I need to follow? How do I do assessment and record keeping?

Students

What proficiency levels are the students at and what English language skills have they attained? Who taught them previously and can I talk to that person? How should I counsel and/or discipline my pupils?

Exploratory Break 1.9
Helping Yourself

Some of these questions may seem obvious, but by posing and attempting to get answers to them, beginning teachers can develop greater awareness for their own professional socialization and take more explicit responsibility for their own professional development. Try to get answers to these questions.

- Can you think of other questions first-year language teachers can ask to better prepare for their first years as a language teacher?

Of course there are other important players in the induction of new teachers, such as the teacher-training program or institution that the teacher has just graduated from and other agencies (such as the Ministry of Education); however, different countries and institutions may have different organizations controlling the selection and placement of teachers. Just because teachers have graduated from an institution, it does not mean that teacher educators should relinquish their responsibilities for ensuring a successful transition for the first-year teacher.

CHAPTER REFLECTION

It is impossible to predict what teaching situations newly qualified English language teachers may find themselves in as the contexts and situations vary from university-based language institutes, to elementary and secondary schools (as in the case study example), to private institutes. As Bullough and Baughman (1993) gladly point out,

> Thankfully, the process of becoming a teacher will always remain wonderfully mysterious despite the best efforts of researchers to achieve control, just as the ends of education inevitably will remain unpredictable, a condition for which we should be grateful. (p. 93)

Nevertheless, teachers of English language in their first years can do much to improve their chances of having a successful transition from the teacher education institution by preparing realistically for what they are about to face in real second language classrooms.

CHAPTER TWO

Planning English Language Lessons

"Would you tell me, please, which way I ought to go from here?" asked Alice. "That depends a good deal on where you want to get to," said the Cheshire Cat (Carroll, 1963). English language teachers in their first years may wonder many times "which way they ought to go" before they enter a classroom to teach a lesson, and this puts extra stress on an already difficult task (see Chapter 1). However, by planning lessons before class (writing them is better than trying to keep them in your head), you can take some of the pressure off, even if the lesson does not go according to plan. Many experienced teachers actually engage in yearly, term, unit, weekly, and daily lesson planning, but of all these, the daily lesson plan is the most important for beginning teachers because the yearly and term plans are often made by the English department of the school (or school district) the teacher is about to teach in. This chapter focuses on the daily planning decisions that English language teachers in their first years should consider before they enter the classroom. I define lesson planning as the daily decisions a teacher makes for the successful outcome of a lesson. This chapter discusses the following issues related to daily lesson planning: why plan lessons, different models of lesson planning, and practical suggestions of how to plan a lesson. I hope that you will see how taking the time to plan before you teach a class can relieve some of the stresses of in-class teaching.

Exploratory Break 2.1
Why Plan Lessons?

- List the advantages of writing lesson plans.
- List the disadvantages of writing lesson plans.
- Will you plan your lessons in writing? Why? Why not?

WHY PLAN A LESSON?

Keeping systematic records of what you will attempt to cover in a lesson will help you think about the lesson in advance and enable you to troubleshoot and anticipate problems before they happen during the lesson. Planning in advance also helps provide some structure for you by giving you a map to follow (Richards, 1998). It can also provide a record of what you have planned, and thus may be important if you are on your first-year probation in a school. The extent of the planning may well determine the success of a lesson. Lesson planning can also provide you with confidence, because these plans may actually help you organize (and even learn) the subject matter better so that the lessons run smoothly. Moreover, should you not be able to teach for whatever reason, a substitute teacher can follow clearly what he or she is required to cover in that particular lesson by reading your lesson plan.

Exploratory Break 2.2
Benefits of Planning Lessons

Think of the benefits of coming into your class with a written lesson plan, and compare your answer to what is presented below. For English language teachers, planning lessons will help you do the following:

- Consider and prepare the content and materials you will use in the lesson.
- Consider how you will sequence and time all the activities you plan.
- Anticipate difficulties with content, materials, sequencing, and timing of activities.
- Provide more security (in the form of a map) for you in the sometimes-unpredictable atmosphere of a classroom.
- Provide you with a log of what has been planned and, if followed, a log of what has been taught.

- Guide a substitute to smoothly take over a class when you cannot teach.
- Benefit your students because the plan can take into account the different backgrounds, interests, learning styles, and abilities of all the students in your class.

MODELS OF LESSON PLANNING

In your teacher education course, you probably studied many different approaches to lesson planning that may or may not have included planning ESL lessons (in my experience, it probably did not include planning language lessons). You may also have realized from these classes that the most talked-about model of lesson planning that still influences what teachers do in their classrooms today, even though it was developed in 1949 is Tyler's rational-linear framework to lesson planning. Yes, it may seem strange to refer back to this classic, but I think it is easier to plan for a clear sequence of events to happen in your class during your first year; when you get more experience, you can experiment with this model in any way that suits your needs. Tyler's model has four sequential steps that are easy for teachers to follow:

1. Specify objectives

2. Select learning activities

3. Organize learning activities

4. Specify methods of evaluation

In fact, many experienced teachers still use this means of planning their lessons, although it is doubtful whether teachers actually present their lessons in such a linear way. In English language teaching, lesson planning is somewhat of a new consideration, as the ESL teacher has not been the focus of research when it comes to planning lessons until relatively recent times (Farrell, 2002). What little research exists suggests that many language teachers rarely stick to the plans they make before the lesson (Richards, 1990). In a detailed case study of an experienced teacher of reading, Richards found that the teacher used instructional objectives to guide and organize the lessons, suggesting that writing these objectives before a lesson can greatly help beginning teachers organize their lessons. How much detail you want to include in these lesson plans depends on how much structure you feel you need. For example, you can plan for promoting specific language skills that are within the functional ability of a student, or students, in a specific skill such as speaking, writing, reading, and listening. You can also plan for specific functions of a student, or students, within a specific content area. Additionally, you can plan for gauging the performance level attained at the end of a course.

Exploratory Break 2.3
Lesson Plan Details

- Do you think you may want to make detailed plans before your lesson?
- Do you feel you may be restricted by planning too much before a lesson?

So, there seems to be consensus among teacher educators that teachers should plan their lessons in some systematic way in order to avoid random, unfocused, and thus unproductive learning. Additionally, the benefit of clearly stated lesson plans will more than likely maintain the attention and interest of your students and minimize confusion about what they can expect during the lesson.

HOW TO PLAN AN ENGLISH LANGUAGE LESSON

Writing actual lesson plans involves three stages of development: developing the plan, implementing the plan, and evaluating the plan.

Developing the Plan

Beginning language teachers may think that preparing a lesson plan is done just before they enter their lesson or the night before the lesson. One reason for considering doing this long before the lesson is that language lessons are unique when compared to content lessons. English language lessons are different from content lessons because teachers may have to reinforce the same content again and again. However, beginning English language teachers may not be experienced enough to recognize this uniqueness.

One of the most important aspects of daily lesson planning is writing lesson objectives, or what a teacher wants to achieve by the end of a lesson. In language teaching, Shrum and Glisan (1994) say that "effective objectives describe what students will be able to do in terms of observable behavior and when using the foreign language" (p. 48). Therefore, the type of language a teacher uses for stating objectives is important. For example, vague verbs such as *understand, appreciate, enjoy,* or *learn* should be avoided because they are difficult to quantify (but may be used for poetry lessons, perhaps). It is best to use action verbs such as *identify, describe, explain, demonstrate, list, contrast,* and *debate*; these are clearer and easier for teachers to design a lesson around. These can be centered on specific skills you are trying to teach, such as knowledge, comprehension, application, analysis, synthesis, or evaluation skills. For example, if your instructional objectives include the promotion of knowledge skills in your lesson, you can get your students to define, identify, list, and so on. If you want to promote comprehension skills, you can have your students explain, summarize, predict, and so on. If you want to promote application skills, then your students will be required to demonstrate, produce, show, and so on. If you plan analysis objectives, then they will be required to select, differentiate, identify, and so on. For synthesizing skills promotion in your classes, students will be required to explain, combine, categorize, and so on. Finally, in order to promote evaluation skills, your students will be required to justify, relate, summarize, explain, and so on. If language teachers write their lesson plans in terms of skills they want their students to learn, then the students themselves may find it easier to understand exactly what will be expected from them in each lesson.

Exploratory Break 2.4
Writing Lesson Objectives

Here are examples of some instructional objectives (what you want your students to achieve by the end of the lesson). See if you can add to this list by writing more objectives.

- To identify between singular and plural nouns
- To describe the features of an essay
- To contrast a narrative text with an expository text

I have found Madeline Hunter and Douglas Russell's (1977) model of lesson planning (again an old one) useful as a general guide for beginning ESL teachers because it plans for a lesson to have five connected sequential phases:

1. Opening phase: The teacher asks the following questions: What was the previous activity (what was previously learned)? Then the teacher gives a preview of the new lesson.

2. Stimulation phase: The teacher poses a question to stimulate students' thinking about the forthcoming activity in an attempt to help them relate the activity to their everyday lives. A great way to get students tuned into a lesson is to begin with an attention grabber such as an anecdote, a little scene acted out by peer teachers or lay assistants, a picture, or a song. This attention grabber can be used as a lead-in to the main activity of the lesson.

3. Instructional phase: The teacher now encourages the students to become as involved as possible in the language lesson during the instructional phase. For example, and depending on the lesson objective, the teacher can build in pair and/or group work to the main activity so the students are all participating as much as possible.

4. Closure phase: Now the teacher summarizes what he or she covered in the lesson and checks for student understanding by asking such questions as "What did you learn?" and "How did you feel about these activities?" During this phase, the teacher gets students' input so they can follow up in future lessons.

5. Follow-up phase: The teacher can give the students opportunities to do independent work or homework to practice what was presented in the lesson.

Although the original Hunter-Russell model was not specifically for language teachers, and was very much teacher controlled, Shrum and Glisan (1994) adapted it for language teachers and suggest that as students gain competence, "they can gradually take on a larger role in choosing the content and even in the structure of the lessons themselves" (pp. 187–188).

Exploratory Break 2.5
Lesson Design

- Look at the following lesson plan template and try to fill it in for a specific lesson you are about to teach.

Lesson Phase	Teacher	Student Responses
1. Opening		
*What have students learned previously?		
*Preview new lesson		
2. Stimulation		
*Prepare students for new activity		
*Present attention grabber		
3. Instruction		
*Present main activity		
*Check for understanding		
*Encourage involvement		
4. Closure		
*Ask what students have learned		
*Preview future lessons		
5. Follow-up		
*Give homework to reinforce same concepts		

Depending on what the focus of the lesson is (e.g., speaking, grammar, writing, reading), there needs to be a period of "practical application," where the teacher engages the students in communicative activities. This is why the follow-up phase, in my opinion, is vitally important for language teachers and learners. Teachers need to prepare their students for the homework they give them.

English language teachers should by now realize that reading, speaking, listening, and grammar will have different types of lessons. I include an example of a lesson plan for an English reading class as Resource A (Farrell, 2002). This is an example of a plan in a specific context and should not be seen as a prescription, or "how-to," because each teaching context will be different.

Exploratory Break 2.6
Questions to Consider Before Lessons

The following questions may be useful for language teachers to answer before planning their lessons:

- What do you want your students to learn in this lesson?
- Why did you choose this focus?
- Are all the activities necessary and pitched at the right level?
- What materials and aids will you use and why?
- How will you group the students and why this way?
- How will you check your students' levels of understanding?
- Can you think of other questions that may be important to consider before teaching a lesson?

Implementing the Plan

The following are guidelines on how to implement lesson plans:

Don't teach the textbook, exploit it.

Know exactly what you want to teach.

Keep the pace of the lesson steady—don't let it drag.

Use a variety of activities to keep interest levels as high as possible.

Build in a few surprises so that the students can't always predict what is to follow.

Don't be afraid to throw away the lesson plan if the lesson takes a different but important direction that you hadn't planned.

Language lessons can get boring for both teachers and students, so variety within the lessons should be considered so that the students can remain focused. Thus we should plan our lessons with classroom management matters in mind (see Chapter 3). Language teachers can consider the following methods of varying and pacing a language lesson so that they have minimum classroom management problems:

- *Tempo.* Decide what balance, between fast moving and slow, you want for the activities in your lessons.
- *Organization.* Decide if you want to have individual, pair, or group tasks, or full class interaction.
  Decide the mode and skill: decide whether you want to focus on written or spoken language and how much of each.

- *Difficulty.* Build in some easy activities along with more demanding activities.
- *Mood.* Build in fun as well as serious activities.
- *Transitions.* Plan for clear transitions between each activity so that they all flow together.

Exploratory Break 2.7
Components of a Language Lesson

Ur (1996, p. 216) has suggested that a language lesson should consist of the following components:

Put the harder tasks earlier.

Have quieter activities before lively ones.

Think about transitions.

Pull the class together at the beginning and the end.

End on a positive note.

- What do you think of these components? Are they useful?
- Try to plan a specific language lesson using these components.

Evaluating the Plan

The final aspect of planning your daily lessons actually happens after the lesson has ended (although evaluation can, and should, take place during the lesson, too!), when the teacher must evaluate the success (or failure) of the lesson. This form of lesson reflection on what worked and what did not work is necessary for development, because without an evaluative component in the lesson, the teacher has no way of assessing the success of the students or what adjustments to make for the next lesson (Brown, 1994). For evaluating language lessons, the first and most important criterion that should be considered is the level of student learning, because that is why we have a lesson in the first place. It may be difficult to know exactly what your students have learned as a result of sitting in your class, but as you gain experience, you will be able to "tell" if they were engaged during the lesson, if they remained on task, if they seemed to enjoy the lesson, and if the lesson seemed to achieve what you had intended.

Exploratory Break 2.8
Questions for Teachers to Consider After the Lesson

The following questions may also be useful for language teachers to reflect on after conducting a lesson. Answers can be used as a basis for future lesson planning:

- What do you think the students actually learned?
- What tasks were most successful? Least successful? Why?
- Did you finish the lesson on time?
- What changes (if any) will you make in your teaching and why (or why not)?

Can you think of other questions that may be important to consider after teaching a lesson?

Exploratory Break 2.9
Questions for Students to Consider After the Lesson

Teachers can give the following questions to their students at the end of each class. The answers to these questions can assist teachers with future lesson planning. I avoid overly judgmental questions such as "did you enjoy the lesson?" as these questions seek highly subjective responses:

- What do you think today's lesson was about?
- What part was easy?
- What part was difficult?
- What changes would you suggest the teacher make?

Can you think of other questions that may be important to consider after teaching a lesson?

CHAPTER REFLECTION

In this chapter, I have focused on the day-to-day lesson planning decisions that face language teachers. For beginning language teachers, the act of having to write down a daily lesson plan is a good exercise in reflection because it is like a road map "which describes where the teacher hopes to go in a lesson, *presumably taking the students along* [italics added]" (Bailey, 1996, p. 18). It is the latter part of this quote that is important for teachers to remember, for as Bailey correctly points out, "Our best laid plans often go astray" (p. 38). We cannot predict what will happen during a lesson, and this is the exciting tolerance for ambiguity language teachers must build up throughout their teaching careers. The key to a successful lesson starts with planning; however, as Bailey points out, "In realizing lesson plans, part of a skilled teacher's logic in use involves managing such departures [from the original lesson plan] to maximize teaching and learning opportunities" (p. 38).

RESOURCE A: LESSON PLAN

Time: 12:00–12:35 p.m.   **Subject:** English Language

Class: Mixed Ability   **Language Focus:** Reading   **Topic:** Sport

Objective: To teach the students to skim to find the main idea of the passage

Prior Knowledge:

Students have learned how to locate information by reading and finding the main sentence of each paragraph. This lesson is to practice increasing their reading speed within scanning and skimming for information.

Materials:

1. Reading materials—article from book on sport

2. Overhead projector/OHTs

3. Whiteboard

Step	Time	Teacher (T) Tasks	Student (S) Tasks	Interaction	Purpose
1	5–10 min.	Opening: Introduction to the topic of sport. T activates schema for sport. T asks students to help him or her write down as many different kinds of sport on the whiteboard within 3 minutes. T asks students to rank their favorite sports in order of importance.	Listen. Ss shout out the answers to the questions as the T writes the answers on the board. T writes the answers.	T ⟷ Ss	Arouse interest. Activate schema for sport.
2	5–7 min.	Teacher distributes handout on sports schedule from the newspaper. T asks Ss to read it quickly and answer the true/false questions that follow it within 3 minutes. T goes over the answers.	Ss read the handout and answer the questions. Ss call out their answers to the T. Ss check their answers.	T ⟷ Ss Ss ⟷ T	Focus attention of Ss on the concept of skimming for general gist with authentic materials.
3	5 min.	T tells students that they just practiced skimming to get the general meaning or gist of a passage. T gives another handout on sport from the textbook (*New Clue*). T asks the Ss to read and answer the true/false questions written on the paper within 5–7 min.	Ss read the handout and answer the questions Ss call out their answers to the T.	T ⟷ Ss Ss ⟷ T (S ⟷ S possible)	Get Ss to read passage quickly to get the overall meaning.

Step	Time	Teacher (T) Tasks	Student (S) Tasks	Interaction	Purpose
		T asks Ss for answers and writes them on the board.	Ss check their answers.	T ←——→ Ss	
4	5 min.	T summarizes the importance of reading a passage quickly first in order to get the gist. T gives homework of reading the next day's newspaper front-page story and writing down in four sentences the gist of the story. **Follow-up:** Next lesson: Teach the students to skim to find the main idea of the passage.		T ←——→ Ss	Remind students what they have just done and why—develop pupil metacognitive awareness.

CHAPTER THREE

Classroom Management

In the previous chapter, we looked at how to plan a lesson, and I suggested that if a lesson is well planned, that is half the battle when it comes to managing the class because you are increasing your chances that discipline will not be an issue. If you have planned what you want to do and how you want to do it, it will be easier for you to organize the learning environment you want to foster in your classroom, and, also, your students will know what is expected from them. Additionally, when your lesson plan includes activities that are used to maximize student-learning time, where activities are meaningful and interesting, students will not usually question your methods or engage in disruptive behavior.

This chapter attempts to prepare you about how to take care of that monumental task of classroom management. However, right from the start, I would like to move away from the business connotation of the word *management* and explain the teacher's job more in terms of conductor of an orchestra. This chapter outlines how teachers in their first years can go about creating a learning environment where ESL students of diverse backgrounds get along and learn how to communicate in English as a second language. The chapter will cover how to monitor and control classroom interaction, how to manage group work, how to manage behavior, and diversity.

Exploratory Break 3.1
Teacher: Manager or Conductor

- Do you see yourself as a "manager" or a "conductor"?

ORGANIZING THE CLASS

As already mentioned, lesson planning is the necessary first step in managing a class, and this happens before you go in. Teachers can plan the opening phase of the lesson, the instructional phase (the main part of the lesson), and how to end the lesson. Hence you should be well prepared to walk in and teach the class. Now you must meet the reality of the classroom. Plans have been made and you must put them into action. However, human beings, and students in particular, do not always react the way we plan for them to react. For example, our students may be tired and restless for any number of reasons. They may have had a difficult class previous to yours or they may have some trouble going on in their personal lives. Regardless of the cause, not every class will go according to your plan. Sometimes you will have to react to what you encounter, such as some students will not participate in activities, some will be difficult to control, some will do all the work in a group while others will do no work, and yet other students will continuously shout answers without giving their peers a chance to answer. So, another important aspect of conducting a class is how you want to organize your classroom and the interaction you want to encourage in your class.

Exploratory Break 3.2
Organizing the Class

Draw your ideal classroom.

- How many different types of interaction can happen in a class?
- Draw all the different ways you see students interacting in your ESL class.

My answer is that students can work alone, in pairs, in small groups, in large groups, or as a whole class. It is always best, however, to balance how you control interaction in your classroom among students working alone, learning in groups (I call this cooperative learning), and whole-class instruction by the teacher. This way, you can have more variety in class, and your students will not always get bored with the same approach to interaction. This section will focus on group work, or cooperative learning, because, in my experience working with new language teachers for the past 27 years, maintaining control of the class during group work may be the most difficult aspect of classroom interaction that teachers in their first years will face.

CONDUCTING GROUP WORK

When considering group work in language classes, I always suggest the idea of taking a cooperative learning approach because there are enormous benefits associated with cooperative learning, such as increasing self-esteem and fostering interpersonal relationships (Slavin, 1995). For ESL students, a cooperative learning approach can provide more time to practice English with a focus on negotiating meaning rather than just talking about the weather. Additionally, this approach includes a larger number of participants in a discussion, thus providing more comprehensible input (Liang, Mohan, & Early, 1998). That said, we must not forget that cooperative learning should be combined with other activities; otherwise, the students may get bored with group work.

Exploratory Break 3.3
Conducting Group Work

Try to answer the following important questions teachers in their first years may have for conducting group work (from Jacobs & Hall, 2002) in language classes. Then compare your answers to what you read in the next paragraphs.

- How big should groups be?
- How should groups be formed?
- When students are working in their groups, how can the teacher get the class's attention?
- What can be done if the noise level becomes too high?
- What if a student doesn't want to work in a group?
- What if some groups finish earlier than others?

How big should groups be? The smaller the group, the more each member talks and the less chance that someone will be left out. Large groups are also good, because they have more students working together to get big tasks completed. However, as Jacobs and Hall (2002) remind us, research on cooperative learning (e.g., Kagan, 1992) recommends groups of four for ease of classroom management, especially for teachers in their first years.

How should groups be formed? It is best if the teacher selects the group members in the beginning, as they can usually achieve more of a heterogeneous mix that promotes peer tutoring and keeps the members focused on the task at hand (Jacobs & Hall, 2002). In ESL classes, you will inevitably have mixed-ability groups, in which some ESL students will be more proficient in English than others, and this factor should also be considered when forming groups. One way I have found successful is to mix the groups with learners of different proficiency levels, as they can help each other with different tasks. For example, some students may have higher language proficiency levels than others; however, the other students may be more skilled at organizing problem solving and thus the group members can cooperate to combine these diverse talents to make a group report. However, I have sometimes noticed that higher-proficiency students may need to be challenged to produce the language at a higher level than would be required if they are working with lower-proficiency students, and, as such, teachers may want to consider requiring more challenging linguistic demands from them in each group. This can be achieved by having the higher-proficiency student act as the group reporter or by getting him or her to take notes about the group's discussion. Occasionally, I form a group with the same (or similar) proficiency levels so that they can challenge each other at their own similar levels of language and not be intimidated (perceived or otherwise) by higher-proficiency students or become disinterested because of lower-proficiency levels of other students in the group. Jacobs and Hall (2002) suggest that when the students have mastered cooperative learning in groups, they could begin to group themselves according to subject interest levels.

When students are working in their groups, how can the teacher get the class's attention? When I want to get the students' attention during an active class discussion, I may do any of the following: flick the lights on and off; whistle loudly; or raise my hand, to which students respond by stopping and raising their hands. For keeping groups thinking about the time allotted for group discussion, I also ask a member in each group to be responsible for keeping the group informed about the passing of time and how much time remains to complete a project.

What can be done if the noise level becomes too high? This is usually not a problem for me as a teacher, but it can be for the teacher in the next classroom or near me. I can use the same signals I mentioned previously to get the class's attention if I think the noise levels are too high. Additionally, one student in each group can be appointed as a noise monitor to keep the noise at acceptable levels (Jacobs & Hall, 2002).

What if a student doesn't want to work in a group? This is a perennial problem for language teachers: what to do about the student who will not cooperate! One reason a student may not want to take part is that he or she may not be used to group work because of a cultural background that does not value group work. Teachers may want to discuss the process in more detail with these students and show how it is beneficial to use "two heads are better than one" to finish some tasks. If, however, they still do not want to work in a group, rather than pushing them into this form of learning and possibly disrupting other groups, it may be best to let them work alone. Who knows, after a period "out in the cold," they may want to join in.

What if some groups finish earlier than others? In my 28 years of teaching, I have never used groups where at least one group didn't finish before all the other groups. This can be a problem for teachers in their first years as, if it is left alone, the early-finishing group can disrupt other groups and the group members can become bored and lose interest in group work. I have found that if each member of the group has an assigned role such as group leader, timekeeper, scribe, or group reporter, then the work is never really finished because, even if the scribe has written the group's opinion, the group must decide how it will be reported. As teachers get more experience with group work, they will learn more about what time limits to set for each task so they can limit the amount of disruption from groups who may finish early.

ELICITING POSITIVE STUDENT BEHAVIOR

Sometimes in ESL classes, especially large classes, some students may tend to get off-task for one reason or another and disengage from the class activities. This can be a dilemma for teachers in their first year because they may not have had any time to build up a repertoire of skills about how to handle the disengaged student.

Exploratory Break 3.4
Dealing With the Disengaged ESL Student

Lewis (2002) has come up with the following cases that challenge ESL teachers to deal with off-task behavior. How would you deal with each case?

- The back-row distracter: The same student sits at the back and distracts other students.
- The nonparticipants: The same students do not participate in class activities.
- The overexuberant student: The same student always shouts out answers or dominates the class.

The Back-Row Distracter

What do you do when the same student sits at the back and continues to distract other students? This can be very disconcerting for you as a new teacher, as you want to be liked by all your students and, if you publicly reprimand the student, you may think you are poisoning the class atmosphere. If you do nothing, though, you can lose control of your own class. So, you have to do something or else you may lose respect from the whole class. Some interesting methods suggested by Lewis (2002) include the following: stare at the disruptive student while continuing to speak, stop speaking and stare at the disruptive student, and/or talk to the disruptive student after the class and lay down the law that this behavior will not be tolerated. I would go further and say to ask the student to leave the room if he or she continues to disrupt your class because it is *your* class and not his or hers. You could also have a class discussion on how to behave and emphasize that misbehavior hurts everyone and so is a waste of time. If you are teaching in a school district in which this is a big problem, why not videotape the students who are causing trouble and invite the parents of the students who are trying to learn to watch the tape and decide what action they want to take.

The Nonparticipant

Another dilemma for new teachers is how to handle the problem of the same students not willing to participate in class activities (the non-participants, as Lewis [2002] calls them). My rule is, if they do not want to learn and they are not disrupting you or other students, leave them alone. However, I would establish certain norms of behavior for these non-participants, such as not letting them put their heads down on the desk to sleep, as this sends the wrong message to other students. As one of my high school teachers used to tell me, "Farrell, please look in the general direction of the book!" Additionally, you can talk to the nonparticipant student and ask what is bothering him or her. Now, again, I tend to take a hard-line position with this problem, and many times I ask the nonparticipant student to leave the room if I can, because he or she tends to dampen the atmosphere for all in the room. It may be a good idea to videotape the nonparticipant and to show this to the parents of the nonparticipant, the parents of the students who want to learn, and, of course, the principal before you ask the student to leave the room. Although many beginning teachers tend to blame themselves if *every* student is not learning, usually you find that it is not *you* at all who is to blame; if you consult other colleagues, you may find that the same students are either disruptive and/or not willing participants in other classes.

The Overexuberant Student

What can ESL teachers do when the same student, the overexuberant student (Lewis, 2002), always shouts out answers without waiting for others to participate or generally dominates the class? This is not an easy dilemma to deal with because you do not want to kill any of the exuberance, especially if telling the student to be silent deflates and demoralizes him or her into a permanent silence. I have found that a quiet talk after the class works to inform the student that there are others in the room who need to practice their English just like him or her and that all must have a chance to answer. Of course, more group work can lessen this problem, too.

As you get to know your students and as you build your repertoire of dealing with the various events that occur in your room, you will be able to come up with your own ways of managing learning in your class.

CONTROLLING CLASSROOM COMMUNICATION

The multicultural makeup of your classroom is also an important factor for new ESL teachers to consider, because both teachers and students interpret classroom activities through their own frames of reference (Barnes, 1976), which are sometimes not the same. In second language education, students already face the difficulty of communicating in a new language. This difficulty is compounded when students' learned ways of talking and other forms of language use do not conform to the patterns of communication expected in classrooms and may, therefore, be misunderstood and unappreciated. Second language educators need to be aware of this and attempt to come to understand and appreciate their students' frames of reference.

Exploratory Break 3.5
Facilitating Classroom Communication

- Do you know the main patterns of interaction that can exist in an Anglo-American classroom (or any other context)?

It is important for new teachers to have a high level of awareness of cultural and linguistic diversity and to be sensitive to individual students—especially in the ways they interact with students, making sure that there is no discrimination. It is also important that new teachers be able to recognize (and change) examples of institutionalized racism if the teacher wants to provide equality of opportunity for all the students. This is no easy task. One way to go might be to compare the patterns of interaction that exist in your classroom to those identified by Susan Philips (1983) when she compared the verbal participation of middle-class Anglo-American classrooms with the Warm Springs Indian Reservation community and developed a useful description of verbal interaction in Anglo-American classrooms as follows:

1. Teacher interacts with all students (most common)—the teacher controls who will talk and when; voluntary student participation is through self-nomination and/or compulsory participation through teacher nomination.

2. Teacher interacts with small groups of students (also common), as in reading groups where the students' participation is generally the result of teacher nomination and required individual performance.

3. Students work individually at their desks and the teacher is available for student-initiated interaction.

4. Students work in small groups to complete specific tasks and the teacher provides direct supervision (more common in higher grades).

Exploratory Break 3.6
Investigating Patterns of Interaction in Your Classroom

You may now want to compare these four characteristics of verbal interaction in the classroom to the verbal interactions that exist in your classroom.

- Audiotape (and/or videotape) your class.
- Transcribe all or parts of the communication—this is the hard part, as it will take time and patience to do this.
- Compare the general style of verbal interaction that you see with the four organizational structures identified by Philips.
- Look for patterns of interaction—who asks all the questions, what kind of questions are these, who answers these questions, what kind of groups did you set up, how did you set them up, and so on. The items one can look at are limitless (for a complete discussion of this, see Farrell, 2004b).

FACILITATING DIVERSITY

New teachers may be surprised when they enter an ESL class and discover the range of students they must teach. How can a new teacher facilitate the language development of such a diverse group of students? Taking advantage of this diversity can be a challenging but rewarding task for the ESL teacher because we get to meet students from so many different ethnic, cultural, religious, and socioeconomic backgrounds, which makes our job exciting.

Exploratory Break 3.7
Facilitating Diversity

Compare your answers to the following questions to what you read below.

- What does diversity mean to you?
- Do you see diversity in your classroom as positive or negative?
- How do you think your students can be diverse when it comes to intelligence, cultural backgrounds, and religion?

Jacobs and Farrell (2002, p. 12) have observed that diversity in second language involves "the mix of students we have in our classrooms in terms of backgrounds, e.g., ethnic, religious, social class and first language, sex, achievement levels, learning styles, intelligences and learning strategies." Differences in gender and cultural backgrounds (including the different ethnic, religious, and social backgrounds of the students) must be a factor when it comes to classroom communication and interaction. I have found this to be the case with my own research on different patterns of classroom communication that exist in classrooms with different ethnic groups (Farrell, 2004b).

Exploratory Break 3.8
Facilitating Different Learning Styles

- Do you think your students all approach learning the same way?
- Do you think that each second language learner in your class has a different learning style?
- Can you identify any different learning styles for students?

Second language learners have different and diverse learning styles (Oxford, 1990), but some teachers and the learners themselves may not be aware of these different styles. Four main types of learning styles that have been identified are verbal, visual, logical, and hands-on. For example, some students may be more verbal than other students, so they can be given more work to do with words such as speaking, writing essays, researching, or using the Internet. Yet other students' learning styles may favor a more visual approach, so they can be given assignments such as drawing and painting, making storyboards (as opposed to writing a story), making videotapes, and taking photographs. Others of your students may be logical in approach and should be given puzzles, equations, and other problem-solving assignments. Some of your students may be more hands-on in approach to their learning, so these should be given assignments that get them moving, such as role-plays and experiments.

Exploratory Break 3.9
Looking Ahead

Just to get you started thinking about your teaching of the different skill areas and your ideas about assessment and your professional development, try to answer the following questions before reading the next chapters of this book.

- What is your theory of teaching writing?
- What is your theory of teaching speaking?
- What is your theory of teaching reading?
- What is your theory of teaching listening?
- What is your theory of language assessment?
- What is your approach to your professional development?

CHAPTER REFLECTION

Teaching, whether ESL or other subjects, is the only profession that has a first day each time we meet new students. Other professions have a first day on the job when they enter a new place, but then they settle into routine for the most part. Teachers, on the other hand, have a first day many times in their career, and even though they have taken many methods courses in their teacher preparation courses, they are still anxious each time they meet new students. This is not a failure of their teacher education programs or courses; rather, it is the reality of the world we live in where the only constant we face is change. Teachers continually find themselves having to deal with new technology or new curriculum initiatives throughout their careers, and this can be stressful. ESL teachers are no different, as they must constantly renew their teaching self. What follows in this book is a detailed methodological guide for ESL teachers in their first year or years (or teachers new to ESL) that takes a stance of theory behind practice. In other words, I do not intend the chapters that follow to be a "bag of tricks" approach to teaching ESL. Rather, I hope that new teachers can look at the theory behind their practice in the chapters that follow. Each skill chapter has a theoretical base, and the activities that are presented are all linked to theory. That way, if an activity does not "work" in your class, you will not panic because you will understand the theory behind the activity and thus will be able to come up with your own bank of activities that suit your context and your students' learning needs.

CHAPTER FOUR

Teaching Grammar

In many countries around the world, the method of teaching second and foreign languages over the years has changed from emphasizing overt grammar instruction in the past (although many teachers still rely on a grammar approach to teaching language today) to a more communicative approach in recent times, where grammar teaching is more incidental and not the focus of a complete language lesson. This communicative approach to teaching the English language suggests the omission of overt grammar teaching in favor of achieving proficiency in English through communicative-type activities in class. Now there seems to be a movement in some countries to question this communicative approach to teaching English (and, in some cases, a call for a reintroduction of grammar instruction) in that students are still making grammar mistakes and this may be linked to lack of explicit instruction in grammar.

Exploratory Break 4.1
Teaching and Grammar

- What method do you think should be used to teach grammar—overt lessons in grammar or more communicative (covert) lessons, in which grammar is not emphasized and using (speaking, writing, reading, and listening to) the language is the focus? Explain your stance.
- To learn English grammar, do you think it is necessary to know grammar terms (e.g., past progressive, passive, countable nouns, etc.)?
- How important do you think it is to do grammar practice exercises in class to learn English?

English language teaching has seen many methodological swings throughout the years such as this: teach grammar, do not teach grammar. These methodological swings have been popular in the teaching of other skill areas, too—writing, speaking, listening, and reading—and, as such, English language teachers in their first years may feel unclear about how to actually teach a class in any of these skill areas. Chapters 4–8 in this book, while discussing past and recent trends in methods associated with teaching the English language skill areas, also provide *specific and well-tested* methods that you, an English language teacher in your first years, can immediately implement so that you will not be too confused with all the different methodological swings. After you gain some experience teaching, you can decide your own approach to teaching the skill areas.

The purpose of this chapter is to briefly review some of the literature on the teaching of English grammar and then suggest some approaches to teaching English grammar that you can implement immediately so that you are not too bewildered with what you hear, see, or read about teaching grammar. The chapter starts with the question of what grammar is, because when many students hear this word, they become anxious and bored because they have not had much success learning the rules of grammar. Also, even English language teachers, when they hear *grammar,* oftentimes run for cover because they fear its meaning. This chapter, hopefully, will bring the fun back to the meaning of the word *grammar* as it offers some unique and interesting methods of teaching grammar rules to reluctant learners.

GRAMMAR

Often, when I mention grammar to people at a party, they respond that their grammar is not always correct; this implies that we are all talking about the same thing when we say the word *grammar.* However, there is not general agreement in linguistic circles about a commonly agreed-on definition for the term *grammar.* In fact, grammar's exact role in ESL lessons is still not commonly agreed on: some say we should teach it (but again, there is no agreement about *how* we should teach grammar), while others say we should never teach grammar in ESL classes because children who learn their first language never take grammar lessons from their caregivers. And on and on the debate goes.

Exploratory Break 4.2
Grammar

- When someone says the word *grammar* to you, what does it mean to you?
- What does the "rules of a language" mean to you?
- Look at the definition of grammar below. Do you agree with it?

We should always ask ourselves what the term *grammar* means to us before we think about teaching it. This is because the grammar we see in books can be different from what native speakers of a language actually use—the rules versus the reality of use. The rules are often set by linguists or grammar experts and outline what tradition dictates grammar should be. This is called prescriptive grammar, whereas how native speakers of a language use the language in real life is called descriptive grammar. This is an important distinction for teachers of English language to consider because we must consider one other type of grammar for our students: pedagogical grammar, the grammar we ask our students to learn. This chapter uses Cross's (1991, p. 26) definition of grammar: "the body of rules which underlie a language." This includes rules that govern the structure of words and rules that govern the structure of clauses and sentences "that are acceptable to educated native speakers" (p. 26).

TEACHING GRAMMAR

The teaching of grammar is usually done in reaction to students' errors— "if you teach grammar overtly, then the students will make fewer mistakes" is the reasoning behind this statement. However, at best, teaching students rules and correcting their every error does not help a language learner avoid errors. At worst, it can impede language production because this attention to errors makes the student focus on form at the expense of communication. So what are second and foreign language teachers to do?

Exploratory Break 4.3
Teaching Grammar

I have used the following questionnaire with beginning English language teachers to help them reflect on how they would teach grammar.

Try to identify how many times you will use a teaching practice to teach grammar. You can use the following key:

0 = Never will use—this is something I will not do in class

1 = Infrequently will use—once a week in the class

2 = Sometimes will use—two or three times a week

3 = Regularly will use—I will do this a lot of times (four or five)

In presenting a grammar teaching point for the first time, I will:

1. Present the teaching point indirectly in the context of spoken and written language, but *will not formally teach it.*

2. Present the teaching point indirectly in the context of spoken and written language and will point out the structure.

3. Review with the students relevant, previously presented grammatical structures.

4. Give the students *several examples* of the teaching point and guide them in *discovering the grammar rule.*

5. Give the students several examples of the teaching point before *supplying them with the grammar rule.*

6. *Not focus on grammar* in teaching English.

7. Base new teaching points on previously presented grammatical structures.

8. Write the grammatical rule on the board (or overhead projector) before explaining it.

Review your answers and consider each question as you continue reading this chapter. Also, ask a colleague to complete this questionnaire and compare your answers.

Some teachers teach grammar because it is easy to teach and easier to test than, say, speaking or writing. Other teachers say the most common reason for teaching grammar is that it gives a system for analyzing and labeling sentences. For decades, however, research has demonstrated that the teaching of grammar rarely accomplishes such practical goals because few students learn the rules of grammar well, and even if they do manage to learn the rules of grammar, many still fail to transfer the grammar they have learned to improve their speaking or edit their writing. In fact, for many students, the systematic study of grammar is not even particularly helpful in avoiding or correcting errors, yet we still "feel" that if we do not teach grammar overtly, then our students will make grammar mistakes.

INDUCTIVE AND DEDUCTIVE GRAMMAR TEACHING

Richards and Renandya (2002, p. 145) have recently suggested that grammar is too important to be ignored by language teachers and that "without a good knowledge of grammar, learners' language development will be severely constrained." They suggest that today the issue is not whether grammar should be taught; rather, the issue is how to teach it in its most effective way: inductively or deductively. Knowledge of these two main approaches to the teaching of English grammar, the *inductive* and the *deductive* approach, will be sufficient for you to survive teaching grammar during your first years. An inductive approach to teaching grammar is seen as a method "in which the students' attention is focused on the structure being learned and the students are required to formulate for themselves the underlying pattern" (Shaffer, 1989, p. 395). Shaffer defines a deductive approach to teaching grammar as one "where, regardless of the timing relative to the practice part of the lesson, students are given an explanation" (p. 396). Deductive teaching of grammar, then, refers to giving the students rules of the grammar item before they are given examples in actual usage.

Exploratory Break 4.4
Inductive and Deductive Grammar Teaching

- Which approach do you subscribe to and why?
- Can you think of other approaches to teaching grammar that may be more useful to you?

So, which approach should we use? According to Shaffer (1989), students should try to infer grammar rules from examples instead of being told explicitly what the rules are. This inductive approach supports work done in cognitive research, which has shown "that discovering rather than being told underlying patterns favorably affects retention" (Shaffer, 1989, p. 401). Also, Willis (1986) says that the best way to teach grammar is not by teaching it at all but by providing students with opportunities to learn it. This focus on opportunities reinforces the notion of end use in meaningful situations. Additionally, Celce-Murcia (1991) has pointed out that grammar is a tool or resource to be used in the comprehension of oral and written discourse rather than something to be learned as an end in itself.

However, there is a body of research that supports the need for explicit (or deductive) study of grammar, and this is borne out by empirical research performed by Harley (1989), Scott (1989, 1990), and Shaffer (1989). Scott (1989, 1990) found that explicit grammar teaching of grammar structures results in improved recall and production of those structures on tests that target the particular grammar points studied. Furthermore, Scott (1990) found that implicit grammar instruction, in which students listen to grammatical structures repeated in a natural context, does not promote learning of these target structures. Larsen-Freeman (1991) cautions teachers about jumping on the bandwagon of pointing to the communicative approach as the answer to all language teaching problems. Larsen-Freeman (citing Eskey) continues, "We used to think that if students learned the form, communication would somehow take care of itself. Now we seem to think that if students somehow learn to communicate, mastery of the forms will take care of itself" (p. 279). In fact, there is little evidence that the communicative approach produces better language students than more traditional approaches that focus on form. So I would say that each teacher in each context, because he or she knows the students' language needs best, should design activities for lessons of English grammar that best suit those needs.

GUIDELINES FOR PREPARING GRAMMAR LESSONS

The following guidelines may be useful to remember when preparing lessons for a grammar class.

• *Know what type of grammar you want to teach in the lesson.* When in doubt, follow descriptive rather than prescriptive grammar rules. Look at how people use the language in their everyday lives and see if it conflicts with the rules you are teaching. Grammar rules will vary depending on such things as meaning, genre, and register. Just look at your computer grammar check and see what it suggests you do regarding *your* use of grammar when you write—is it always correct? I think you'll agree it is not. Also, remember that grammar rules will change over time, so what you see in a textbook should be constantly compared to what is used outside the classroom by society.

• *Time and plan your grammar lessons.* Have a clear lesson plan to make a clear transition from one grammar activity to the next. You may want to consider presenting a grammar item in the middle of a lesson, but this all depends on which approach you take (inductive or deductive). For example, grammar-focusing techniques can be embedded in meaningful, communicative contexts.

• *Decide on how much grammar metalanguage you want to introduce in each lesson.* Do your students need to know *all* the grammar terminology? That is a question only you can answer, and your answer will depend on your position about grammar in language learning. My suggestion would be to try not to overwhelm students with grammar terminology—bring the terminology in slowly like a foreign language.

• *Let the students help with the construction of the grammar lessons.* Try to produce English language grammar lessons where teachers and learners "collaborate on and co-construct the grammar explanations" (Shrum & Glisan, 1994, p. 92), where both contribute to the success of the lesson. I think that inductive grammar lessons would be most suitable for this.

Regarding the last guideline mentioned, the strategic methods presented in the next section have this "coconstruction" as a main focus of teaching English grammar. Regardless of what approach the so-called experts say teachers should take, it is each individual teacher who should decide day-by-day and class-by-class which approach would benefit their students.

A STRATEGIC APPROACH TO TEACHING GRAMMAR

How, then, should we teach grammar? Should we teach the rules and hope that the students learn these rules and are able to apply them to constructions of English they may come up with in their written compositions and their spoken presentations? This may seem logical, but read the following poem in Exploratory Break 4.5 (by an unknown author) and see how illogical the rules of the English language really are.

CRISP GRAMMAR ACTIVITIES

So, where does a poem like this leave the confused teacher of English? The above poem clearly shows that the rules of English grammar do not follow

Exploratory Break 4.5
Why Is English So Hard?

Read the following poem:

We'll begin with a box, and the plural is boxes;
but the plural of ox should be oxen not oxes.
Then one fowl is goose, but two are called geese;
yet the plural of moose should never be meese.

You may find a lone mouse or a whole lot of mice.
But the plural of house is houses not hice.
If the plural of man is always called men,
Why shouldn't the plural of pan be called pen?

The cow in the plural may be cows or kine,
but the plural of vow is vows, not vine.
And I speak of a foot, and you show me your feet,
but I give you a boot—would a pair be called a beet?

If one is a tooth and a set are teeth,
why shouldn't the plural of booth be beeth?
If the singular is this, and the plural is these,
should the plural of kiss be nicknamed kess?

Then one may be that, and three may be those,
yet the plural of hat would never be hose.
We speak of a brother, and also of brethren,
but though we say mother we would never say mothren.

The masculine pronouns are he, his, and him,
but imagine the feminine she, shis, and shim.
So our English, I think you would agree,
is the trickiest language you ever did see.

—Anonymous

- Can you explain the rules of grammar from reading this poem?
- Look at each verse and try to write the grammar rule and exceptions to this rule.

a logical application. I think that both approaches can be integrated into one where student attention is, as Shaffer (1989) says, "focused on grammatical structure used in context so that students can consciously perceive the underlying patterns involved" (p. 395). It is with this in mind that I present two methods that incorporate the best of both inductive and deductive approaches: the *peanut butter sandwich approach* and *conversation aboard a jet*. Both methods are what I call CRISP: Clear, Relevant, Interesting, Short, and Productive.

The two methods presented in this chapter follow Brown's (1994) ideas when he says that "appropriate grammar focusing techniques are embedded in meaningful, communicative contexts; contribute positively to communicative goals; promote accuracy with fluent communicative language; do not overwhelm students with linguistic terminology; are lively and intrinsically motivating" (p. 349). Also, the methods take up Shrum and Glisan's (1994) concept of "guided participation" where "teachers and learners collaborate on and co-construct the grammar explanations" (p. 92).

Peanut Butter Sandwich Approach

Method

The teacher starts the class by taking out a jar of peanut butter and a knife and two slices of bread. He or she then proceeds to put peanut butter on the knife and then on one side of one of the slices of bread. The teacher then asks the class what he or she is doing, thus practicing the present continuous tense. The class answers. The teacher then asks the class what he or she just did, thus practicing the past tense. The class answers. The teacher goes on to make a sandwich, always stopping to ask what he or she was doing and what he or she just did, reinforcing the meaning of the present continuous tense and the past tense rather than teaching these tenses explicitly, as is usual in many English classes. When finished, the teacher gives out a handout (following this paragraph) for the students to answer. This handout can then be used as a diagnostic device and/or a means of "teaching" tenses from meaning. I have done this in my grammar module classes for secondary English teachers and, believe me, nobody was sleeping. At the end of the exercise, the teacher may eat the sandwich in class. Homework can be for the students to bring in the ingredients of their favorite sandwich and go through the same steps outlined above in pairs to practice whatever tenses or items of grammar the teacher wants to teach.

This approach is CRISP. The presentation of the sandwich by using actual bread and peanut butter and making a sandwich in class is Clear. The

Handout on Peanut Butter Sandwich

Fill in the blank with a suitable word.

A teacher (t   ) us that he would make a sandwich.

First of all, he (p   ) peanut butter on the bread.

He asked us, "What am I (   ) now?"

We said, "You are (   ) peanut butter on the bread."

Next, he asked us, "What (   ) I just do?"

We said, "You (   ) some peanut butter on the bread.

Next, he placed another slice of bread on top of the other slice.

He asked us, "What (   ) I doing?"

We answered, " You are (   ) a slice of bread on top of the other slice.

Then he asked us what he just (   ).

We answered, "You just (p   ) another slice on top of the bread.

He said, "This is the way (   ) (m   ) a peanut butter sandwich!

Finally, he (   ) the sandwich.

students have not much difficulty understanding what you are doing or how to answer the questions. It is also Relevant to the students, although I cannot say for sure that all students will have tasted and liked these sandwiches. I can say, however, that no student will sleep in the class when the teacher starts by taking out bread, a knife, and some peanut butter. Even the student with his or her head surgically attached to the wall will move when the teacher starts to make a sandwich in class and then eats it. So, this is Interesting. The whole process takes 10–15 minutes. Therefore, it is Short. It is also Productive, as they will fill in the worksheet after the event of making a sandwich. It will be even more productive if they can duplicate the process for making their favorite sandwich, which can be assigned for homework. Therefore, the success of this activity is when the students are able to use grammar outside the class and not for achieving "their score on discrete-point grammar tests" (Brown, 1994, p. 353).

Exploratory Break 4.6
Grammar Activity Using the CRISP Method

- Design additional activities based on how the activity above was outlined—you could design an activity using a banana sandwich for past tense practice.
- How would you teach this grammar activity in a traditional approach (e.g., stating the rules first)?

Conversation Aboard a Jet

Method

The grammar focus of this method is English articles. It is a conversation on an airplane between two passengers with all the articles omitted. Unlike most exercises that practice use of articles, however, this method does not provide blanks for the students to fill in. There are two reasons for this:

1. The blank alerts the student that an article is omitted; therefore, the student does not know why the article should be placed in that particular place in the sentence and, thus, does not learn the true meaning of the use of articles.

2. So, in the method presented in this paper, the student must *first* be able to recognize that an article has been omitted and *only then* fill in the proper article.

Exercises that use blanks to indicate a missing article *only* practice usage of articles, not their meaning. The handout (in the boxed text) should be done orally with the students. This can be in the form of a role-play in which the class is split into two sides and one side plays one role and the other side plays another role. Also, each teacher must decide whether he or she needs to teach articles deductively before, during, or after this exercise; it all depends on what the students already know about English article usage.

This method is also CRISP: it is Clear for the teacher and is definitely Relevant for everyday English usage; it is also Interesting because of the humor of the content (which can be adjusted); and it is Short and, hopefully, Productive for both teachers and students. Teachers should also note that more than one answer can be correct. Therefore, teachers should explain the different meanings that can result from inserting *a* versus *the*. For example, consider this sentence:

Why do you always take *a/the* plane? Because *an/the* airplane is fast?

What is the answer? Well, depending on the place, time, people involved, and other events, both could be used. Sometimes you cannot use either form without great confusion.

Exploratory Break 4.7
Create Your Own Grammar
Activities Using the CRISP Method

- Design additional (your own) activities based on how the CRISP method was outlined. You could design a handout with all the verbs missing (no blanks) and ask your students to suggest where they are missing and what would be suitable.
- How would you teach the grammar activity on articles outlined previously in a traditional approach (e.g., stating the rules first)?

CHAPTER REFLECTION

Grammar is sometimes considered a "dirty" word in second and foreign language teaching settings because of the huge swings in teaching methodology in the past from an emphasis of teaching grammar as *the*

Handout on Articles

Conversation Aboard a Jet:

Exercise on the use of A, AN, and THE

Fill in the proper word. In many cases, more than one correct word is possible.

Main characters: **T**: Tom, **G**: Grandma

T: Why do you always take plane? You could take boat if you wanted to, could not you?

G: This is first time I have ever been on plane. Boat might sink.

T: What strange decision! Okay! boat can sink, but plane can crash! It could happen on this plane. We are sitting directly over gas tanks of plane, and if there is explosion . . .

G: What? We are sitting over gas tanks? But I read in book about jets that they have gas tanks in wings. Oh! Let us change subject. . . . Excuse me (to stewardess). Would you bring me whiskey?

(Later)

G: Look out window! These must be lights of New York. How beautiful! What beautiful sight!

T: Do you think I am idiot? Lights of New York? Granny, we are over Australia, heading for city of Sydney! How can you see lights of New York? Maybe we are passing over ship.

G: No! Look for yourself, what beautiful sight! These are brightest lights I have ever seen.

T: Move over, Granny . . . let me take look for myself. (Looks out windows.) Oh . . . Oh! Stewardess! Stewardess! Wake up pilot and copilot and tell them that Numbers 3 and 4 engines are on fire.

language class to more communicative lessons where grammar is not even discussed. It may be a good idea for teachers in their first years to wait before jumping on any particular bandwagon (to teach or not to teach grammar) that espouses an approach that favors one over the other until they have tried both. In other words, they should teach grammar overtly and see what happens and then teach the same language lesson without emphasizing grammar and see what the results of both are. This chapter takes a middle position: that inductive grammar lessons can achieve raising students' awareness level of grammar while providing a more authentic and communicative focus for the students. Nevertheless, it seems that we will always have a certain amount of controversy when the issue of teaching English grammar comes up.

CHAPTER FIVE

Teaching Writing

People write for many different purposes. In school, students write for academic reasons, especially when they are assigned a term paper or an essay, and they also write when they want to take notes in a class. Outside school, people write in their jobs, and they also write to communicate with each other either formally or informally, such as writing a letter to a friend. Consequently, the audience for a piece of writing will be influenced by the purposes of the writing. For example, a teacher who assigns an essay will be the main audience for that essay, at least in the eyes of the students, whereas the public will be the main audience for a letter to the newspaper. A scholar who writes for a specific journal will have in mind a certain group of academics who tend to read such journals. Thus the purpose and audience will also influence the style of writing, which can take the form of formal academic- or professional-style writing or a more informal style such as letter writing or electronic mail communications. This chapter discusses writing in general and how to teach English writing, especially in settings where students need to produce an acceptable piece of academic writing for both their teacher and peers as audience. The chapter outlines two different methods of teaching writing and proposes a modified process approach for teaching English writing for teachers in their first years. When you gain more teaching experience, you can reflect on and revise this modified process approach and modify it again to best suit your own individual context.

Exploratory Break 5.1
Writing

- What is writing to you?
- Do you write often? If yes, what kind of writing do you do?
- Who do you write to? Why?
- If no, why don't you write often?

WRITING

First of all, writing is not an isolated act in which we lock ourselves away in some room like Marcel Proust, who saw writing as a "secretion of one's innermost self, done in solitude, for one's self alone" (Rodby, 1990, p. 42). We usually write because we have something to say to other people, an audience.

Exploratory Break 5.2
Purpose and Audience

- List the different reasons people write.
- List the different types of audiences people write for.
- Now compare your lists to what is presented below.

Techniques such as peer writing and writing in groups provide contexts where second and foreign language writers can communicate to each other about writing and also get a sense of awareness of audience. Suppose you have students from an Asian country taking your English writing class; are you aware that research has shown that some classical Asian texts have a reader-responsible orientation, whereas English has a writer-responsible orientation (Conner & Kaplan, 1987)? This means that many Asian students may have prior writing experiences that are different from what is required in your classroom. They may, for example, expect the reader to be responsible for making sense of the text rather than taking responsibility themselves for mapping out ideas in a clear, coherent, and linear manner. They may write the text in a circular argument style, never fully making their thesis statement clear to the reader, because that is their writing tradition. So, writing as a physical act, like most physical acts, can be performed with (or without) skill. That means that anyone can learn how to write, but they may need a lot of practice and thus help from a teacher.

WRITING AS PRODUCT AND PROCESS

The history of teaching English language writing, especially second and foreign language writing, is littered with giant swings of the methods pen dulum from, on one side, overtly teaching grammar as the basis for composition class with the underlying principal that this will be automatically transferred to the students' writing, to, on the other side, not teaching grammar at all during the writing class. These two different approaches have been called the product approach and the process approach.

WRITING AS PRODUCT

The basic assumption behind this view of writing is that students will focus on producing an accurate composition and that this product reflects the student's competence as a writer. Teachers emphasize grammar and vocabulary and teach them overtly in a product-oriented writing class with the objective that this instruction will help students write clearly in the second or foreign language. The teachers provide models of good writing for their students to follow so that they can avoid errors, but if they do make errors, the teacher will correct these while all the time emphasizing accurate grammar, correct sentence structure, spelling, punctuation, and writing structures. In the product approach, the content of the writing is not as important as the mechanics because the goal of teaching writing is to teach students to produce replicas of the types of texts they will most encounter in their lives: persuasive writing, argumentative writing, narratives, expository writing, and so forth.

Exploratory Break 5.3
Writing as Product

- Now that you have read about writing as product, try to list some disadvantages of this approach.
- Compare your list with what you read below.

One of the main problems with this approach is that it focuses on accuracy in grammar and structure while overlooking the process of writing itself, including the strategies the students used in getting to the final draft. In other words, if students make mistakes, they do not realize why they made them and, in many cases, they continue to make many of the same mistakes again. Additionally, the writing process is very much controlled from beginning to end, and thus students are "stuck" within only what models and structures they have been taught to memorize. They do not learn how to create their own piece of writing. However, an alternative approach, the process approach, looks at how people develop a piece of writing from beginning to end product, and examines how good writers go about this task.

WRITING AS PROCESS

The basic assumption behind this view of writing is that students will slowly develop their thoughts and writing in a process that includes planning, drafting, revising, and editing (Seow, 2002). Peers are encouraged to help each other at different stages of the writing process. Teachers help the writer revise the various drafts and the originality of the student's content is seen as important. Teachers usually look at all the drafts from beginning to the final product when evaluating a composition. Within the process approach, students are taught to consider the audience and purpose of the writing, and they plan a piece of writing with these two in mind from the beginning as they draft, write, and rewrite. Students are encouraged to reflect on their own writing behaviors while deciding to write about topics they are interested in. A detailed example of the process approach in action is outlined in the next section.

Exploratory Break 5.4
Writing as Process

- Now that you have read about writing as process, try to list some disadvantages of this approach.
- Compare your list with what you read below.

One of the main problems with this approach, as mentioned by students, is that they do not have any models to follow when writing and that they have a difficult time trying to find their "voice." They find the product approach easier to follow because they are guided more than in the process approach.

GUIDELINES FOR PREPARING WRITING LESSONS

The strategic process approach that is outlined in this chapter takes the following guidelines into consideration for planning writing lessons.

- *Have students write multiple drafts.* Most writing is not done in one sitting. The writer should get up and walk away and come back later and work on the paper; a writer needs distance away from the paper. This can be built into the classroom teaching of composition by having students take breaks while doing rough drafts. We must remind our students that most writing does not begin at the beginning and proceed to the end. Writing is messy: we get new ideas all the time, we change our minds and direction, and this is fine. Sometimes the beginning of a piece of writing is very different from the final product.

- *Have students share their writing.* Most writing requires intervention. Writing is collaborative and another person or persons (peer, teacher, and parents) can provide valuable input.

- *Explain the writing process in detail to the students.* Most writing goes through multiple rewrites and revisions. This is a fact of life for professional writers, so teachers should teach their students that this is a normal process instead of expecting a perfect final product. However, constraints in the school policy regarding writing assignments must be considered. Thus it may only be possible to perform two revisions of each assignment.

Seow (2002) suggests that teachers should not just tell their students what to do at each stage of the process; rather, they should *show them how to do it by modeling each stage* (teacher modeling).

- *Writing lessons should involve writing.* This guideline may sound obvious, but I have seen writing classes where the teacher only talked about writing or the writing class turned into a grammar class in which students were berated for grammar mistakes in their writing. A writing class should have the students practice some aspect of writing in each class. For example, they could practice writing introductions, conclusions, paragraph topic sentences, or thesis statements in one class.

A STRATEGIC APPROACH TO TEACHING WRITING

As mentioned in the previous section, the original product approach mainly consisted of teacher-assigned topics for students to write about in an unsupervised manner. Typical lessons consisted of grammar practice and vocabulary practice related to the topic. Students were then expected to go home and write a draft, then submit it to the teacher for correction. The teacher then corrected the composition, usually focusing on form (grammar), not content, and usually with a red pen. Students were typically not required to rewrite the composition. This focus on the end product was drastically changed to an approach in which the process of writing the composition from the beginning stage to the end was emphasized. In the beginning stages, both teacher and students brainstormed topics in class; then multiple drafts were required; then feedback was given after each draft, usually focusing on the content; and only when the draft was in its final stages did form become an issue.

Exploratory Break 5.5
Teaching Writing

- Why do we need to teach writing?
- How can students benefit from formal writing lessons?
- What type of writing do our second or foreign language students need?
- Can you name any different approaches to teaching writing to ESL and EFL students?

The approach presented here is a refined process approach from L1 (first language) writing research. It is refined in two ways:

1. First language writers are different than second language writers in that second language writers have the dual task of learning English and learning to write in English. This means that different teaching strategies will be necessary to give more instruction in generating, organizing, and revising ideas (Raimes, 2002).

2. The rhetorical traditions of the various culture groups have to be accounted for in some consciousness-raising techniques. This means that a purely process-type approach, that does not focus on the final product, would have to be adjusted to include both a process orientation and a textual orientation that do not exclude each other (Leki, 1991c).

The strategic process approach has two main assumptions when teaching writing: writing is a process of discovery and errors are inevitable in writing.

WRITING IS A PROCESS OF DISCOVERY

Writing is a process of discovery in which second and foreign language writers should try to understand their own composing process. This can be accomplished by prewriting—gathering, exploring, and organizing material; drafting—structuring ideas into a piece of linear discourse; rewriting and revising; and editing and proofreading. During this process, the students are given time to write and rewrite.

ERRORS ARE INEVITABLE IN WRITING

Many second and foreign language students tend to be obsessed with the terror of making an error to the extent that they can think of nothing else. Consequently, I suggest that you have a discussion about how your students view making a mistake and, more important, how you view different types of mistakes. This can be done on the first day of class so as to check students' anxiety levels concerning the nature of errors. This will go a long way toward relaxing the students and motivating them to try regardless of making mistakes (Leki, 1991b). Ferris (1995) has suggested that teaching students to edit independently in the process approach classroom involves focusing students' attention on their own language mistakes. Students need to be taught that errors can change meaning. Additionally, Ferris suggests that students be given handouts and instruction on error types so they can recognize errors and record their frequency and type in a student journal. As a result, students can use their knowledge of errors to edit their own texts.

Exploratory Break 5.6
Assumptions About Writing

- Do you agree that writing is a process of discovery?
- Do you agree that writing is a social construct?
- Do you think errors are an inevitable part of the writing process?
- Explain your answers to each question.

METHOD

Figure 5.1 outlines the sequence of class events. It should be noted that in the six-stage cycle presented, the revision process can continue on after the final draft (Stage 6), when students get their teacher's feedback on their final drafts. As teachers of English writing, we all know that there is no such thing as a finished piece of writing, so students can be encouraged to rewrite their teacher-commented final drafts for an increase in the original mark given the composition.

Figure 5.1   Six-Stage Cycle

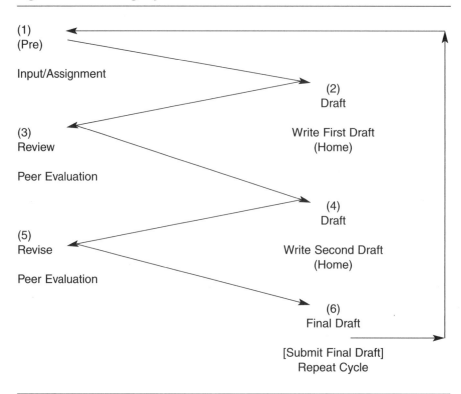

Stage 1: Input (Prewriting)

Input sessions consist of idea-generating activities to help the students focus on the assignment. This approach also recognizes that in some schools, teachers may be obliged to give predetermined writing assignments—such as picture compositions and functional writing. However, even if the teacher chooses the type of assignment, it is also possible for each individual student himself or herself to decide the focus of the assignment (Leki, 1991a), thus ensuring more responsibility and ownership of the piece of writing. Ideas for a topic to write about are generated by one or all of the following means:

Brainstorming. This is where individuals, pairs, or groups speak or write a number of possible topics and then write them on a piece of paper. Each pair or group reviews the list and, by a process of elimination, arrives at a shortlist of topics to write about; however, the final choice for a specific topic is left to the individual writer.

Freewriting: After brainstorming, students can be encouraged to engage in a period of freewriting. Here, the students are required to write as much as possible within a short period of time (usually 15 minutes), without focusing on correctness of grammar, sentence structure, or composition mechanics. The pairs, groups, and so on, can then read each other's work and advise or suggest an alternative focus for the story, not the grammar.

Stage 2: First Draft

Audience awareness is the focus of this stage, with discussions about the different rhetorical traditions and expectations highlighted. Students are asked to write their first draft at home and further develop the ideas generated in the first stage. Of course, students are free to throw out these ideas for some new focus if they so desire.

Stage 3: Peer Evaluation (Review)

Mendonca and Johnson (1994) have suggested that peer review activities are beneficial to second and foreign language students when revising their writing. Students should take the advice of their reviewers most of the time and even appreciate the importance of the feedback reviewers provide. Reviewers have a chance to use their knowledge of writing in a way that promotes learning from their own advice. It is important to stress, however, that students need direct instruction on how to peer review. It is not a good idea, as happens in many writing classes, when the teacher just asks peers to read the essay without any guidelines. This frustrates both the reader (who has no idea what to look for) and the writer (who considers it a waste of time).

Exploratory Break 5.7
Peer Evaluation

- Do you think it is useful to have peers evaluate each other's essays? Explain your answer.
- What guidelines would you offer when setting up peer evaluation in your writing class?

For peer evaluation in this modified strategic approach, students are asked to work in pairs or groups and follow the guidelines given in two handouts. The first handout (on the following page) is for the writer to analyze his or her draft before and after the group sessions.

Handout 1: Personal Reflection: Peer Response Guide for Reviewing Drafts

Before Group Session

1. Write down what you think are the strengths of this draft (the best ideas).

2. What are the weaknesses of this draft (what are you unsure about)?

After Group Session

1. Summarize the most essential contributions of your group.

2. List the changes you plan to make in the draft.

The second handout (below) is for the peer to review the writing.

Handout 2: Peer Evaluation: Written Feedback

Answer the Following Questions About Your Partner's Draft

1. Can you find the writer's main idea? Write the main idea.

2. Can you suggest any further development the writer should do?

3. Have you learned anything new from reading this paper? If you have, tell the writer about it.

4. Write some positive comments about this paper.

> ## Exploratory Break 5.8
> ## Peer Editing
>
> - Do you think both handouts are comprehensive enough for peers to edit each other's drafts?
> - Can you suggest any further questions that may be useful to ask peers about their writing?

I like using peer evaluations in my writing classes because it is good to get students to talk about their own writing and about other students' writing. This reinforces the idea of audience and provides a different audience (from the teacher) than would be possible in the artificial environment of the classroom. Also, two heads may be better than one when it comes to offering ideas for revision; the group may offer better ideas than if the student worked alone. The idea of peer evaluation is also important in a process approach to writing because students themselves must be able to articulate their own opinions of their writing to someone else, besides the teacher, without the fear of being "graded." At this stage in the modified strategic approach to writing, teachers can monitor (from a distance) their students' and peers' opinions of their writing in order to see where the students may have false perceptions of their piece of writing. One way of "monitoring" these perceptions is by collecting all the peer group editing comments at the final draft stage.

Stage 4: Second Draft

Students are encouraged to make changes in the content (or even start over) as a result of the feedback received in the previous stage. Students are then required to write a second draft at home and bring it to the following class.

Stage 5: Peer Evaluation (Revise)

At this stage, students are asked to complete another handout (the same as Handout 2). This handout is to help prepare the class for discussion and to keep the group focused.

Stage 6: Final Draft/Input

The final draft is submitted along with notes from the previous drafts. This is the end of one cycle and the beginning of the next. At this stage of the process, the teacher reads, comments, and returns the composition to the students the following week. However, most teachers only focus on grammar at the expense of meaning, so teachers must be careful to stay with the process approach, which encompasses more than just grammar correction.

GIVING FEEDBACK

Feedback is important to your students, but we haven't yet explored which is the most effective type of feedback to provide on our students' essays.

Exploratory Break 5.9
Feedback

- What kind of feedback should we give English language students on their writing?
- How often should we provide feedback?
- In what manner should we provide this feedback—in writing or orally?

Feedback should provide advice and encourage rather than discourage our students, and Myles (2002) has observed that the process approach can only work if instructors give students feedback concerning their errors and if the students themselves have enough knowledge of the target language to revise their papers. But what exactly is an error, or what is a mistake, for that matter? I have made errors in my writing and will continue to do so, but I would not say that I do not know how to write. Was I going too fast, or thinking ahead, or focusing on something else as I wrote? Probably all of these combined so that I made a mistake. Yes, I used a different term because, when I make a mistake, I can usually correct it myself, but when our language students make an error, it is because they are breaking new language ground and using language they do not normally use and in a way they are not familiar with. One way of finding out all the different errors possible in writing is to gather samples of your students' writing during your first year and document all the different types of errors you find. This way, you can see what your students' needs are in terms of providing the most effective feedback so that they can improve their writing.

Additionally, if our students have sufficient knowledge of the target language and its grammatical structures, it allows them to understand our comments so that they can revise their essays. However, if our learners are not yet proficient in English, then their revisions will tend to be only superficial. In addition, first language transfer can sometimes help students but other times hinder them. Teachers, if they attempt to analyze errors and identify the reasons behind the errors, can give appropriate feedback based on their individual students' needs. With teacher attention to error feedback and students' sufficient language knowledge, learners can thus succeed in process writing.

Feedback can be provided by the teacher throughout the process presented above and whenever the students request it. This feedback can take the form of a checklist returned to the student (see Handout 3).

It is important to realize that feedback on writing means more than just circling all the grammatical errors in an essay and making comments such as "develop more," which I have seen many times. The Handout 3 checklist acts to further reinforce the nature of writing as a process by having only one section on the list (Item 7) for feedback on grammar and mechanics. Teachers tend to be prescriptive in the nature of their written comments, and this denies students a sense of ownership of their work— "I will do what the teacher wants me to do" syndrome. In fact, all the handouts I present in this chapter add to the idea of writing as a process, and this final checklist sees the organization of the composition as being more important than having correct grammar—which is an editorial phase in the writing process, and comes at the end.

Exploratory Break 5.10
The Place of Grammar

- How should teachers of writing handle grammar?
- Should teachers correct every grammar mistake or focus on a few? Explain.
- Should teachers teach grammar structures in a writing class? Explain.

Myers (1997) suggests that process writing has allowed L1 teachers to open their students' writing to the ongoing processes of revision and editing. In order to flesh out second language learners' topics, they need different instruction; second language learners need more practice with the language than L1 writers. Teachers need to couple the process approach with a development of language structures and forms. More clearly, if writing can be seen and taught as a process, grammar, too, can

Handout 3: Writer's Checklist

These are areas where your paper is

	Weak	*Average*	*Strong*
1. **Use of Examples to Support Opinion**			
2. **Ideas Related**			
3. **Logical Order of Ideas**			
4. **Introduction**			
5. **Conclusion**			
6. **Vocabulary**			
7. **Grammar and Mechanics**			

be instructed as a process. This can be achieved through an adaptation of reformulation. Reformulation originally meant that teachers rewrote the students' work to maintain their words and meanings while creating nativelike syntax and structure. Instead of rewriting all, teachers focus on those errors that are most problematic. Through repetition of correct structures, students can learn these structures. However, students don't only receive their teacher's reformulations but also work on their own editing and revision as well.

CHAPTER REFLECTION

Writing is a skill that can be learned and thus taught. However, second and foreign language students may have a different opinion of this, with many thinking that writing is the same as speaking on paper. This could not be further from the truth, as we do not build in turn taking, repair, hesitations, and so on into our writing. Additionally, we must organize it according to certain conventions such as spelling, organization, and grammatical accuracy. A general process approach (with modifications for context and the needs of both teacher and students) may be a good means for second and foreign language students to learn the skill of writing, because they are encouraged to reflect on every step of the writing process: from brainstorming, to initial outline, to each draft, to the final draft. In this way, second and foreign language students can come to realize that writing is not just a finished product but also a process of discovering their own thoughts. Each step of the way toward a final composition can thus be documented and placed in a student's portfolio (see Chapter 9 on language assessment for more on portfolio assessment) that students can self-access to see not just the product of their writing (a composition) but also the process of composing it.

CHAPTER SIX

Teaching Speaking

One of the main sources of evidence of language competency is the ability to speak the language you are learning, but this is easier said than done! In fact, it is more difficult to speak a language than it is to read or listen to it (even though we also must speak in interactive listening situations—see Chapter 8 on listening), because the latter two skills are more receptive, whereas speaking is a productive skill (as is writing, but we have more time to think when we write a second or foreign language). When we are required to produce anything, we generally feel more pressure because we show who we are by the way we speak (or write). Also, when we speak, we must do this instantaneously and interactively with another person or people. This means we have less time to react to what another says or what we say even if we make mistakes when we speak. This chapter outlines some different perspectives of speaking a second or foreign language and how it can be taught in strategic ways.

Exploratory Break 6.1
Speaking a Second or Foreign Language

- What does it mean to be able to speak a language—first and second or foreign language?
- Can you speak a second or foreign language?
- If yes, how did you learn to speak it?
- Do you think a teacher of second or foreign languages has an advantage if he or she speaks a second or foreign language? Why or why not?
- Is it more important to be able to speak a language with accuracy (grammatically correct) or with fluency (communicatively correct, but not always grammatically correct)? Explain your answer.

- What is the difference between speaking and listening to a language?
- Do you think we can teach students to speak a second or foreign language?

SPEAKING

Generally, people speak in order to communicate to each other whether they want to exchange information or just chat about nothing in particular. They may want to exchange information about something specific with one or more people, or they may just want to keep socially active by exchanging pleasantries with friends, neighbors, or working colleagues. Both of these reasons for speaking with others are important, and some would say equally important. When people want to exchange specific information with others, they focus on what they want to say, the specific message they want to convey. The message here is everything and is more important than the messenger, the person who speaks it. Whereas when they want to just maintain social relations by chitchatting, the focus is on the participants in the conversation and their feelings and needs rather than any specific message. In other words, the messenger takes more importance than the message. These two purposes for engaging in conversations have been called interactional and transactional reasons for speaking (these will be discussed in more detail in Chapter 8, "Teaching Listening").

For the purposes of this chapter, I define spoken language as the face-to-face interaction between two or more people. This type of interaction has certain conventions: rules, procedures, and features that distinguish it from other language skill areas (Richards, 1990).

Exploratory Break 6.2
Rules of Face-to-Face Interaction

- List as many rules as you can that you think must be followed by people interacting in face-to-face conversations, and compare them with what you read next.

Shumin (2002) has suggested that because second language students have their own cultural norms that may interfere with English, it may be difficult for them to choose appropriate forms of speech for different situations. This is because each language system has its own rules for speech, and the norms of face-to-face interaction differ in each culture. The following dimensions of conversation (from Richards, 1990) have been identified as important facets of face-to-face interactions, and most people must learn to become communicatively competent within each when speaking a language. If teachers of a second or foreign language can become aware of these three dimensions, they can have a clearer understanding of what it means to participate in a conversation, and this increased awareness can be helpful when preparing speaking lessons. These three dimensions are the following:

1. Turn taking

2. Topics

3. Repair

Because people must speak to each other, it would be impossible if everyone talked at the same time: sometimes we listen, and other times we speak. In other words, we take turns to speak and to listen if we want to have a cooperative conversation (Sacks, Schegloff, & Jefferson, 1974).

Exploratory Break 6.3
Turn Taking

- What is your understanding of turn taking in a conversation?
- How do people allow others to join a conversation in a first language?
- What aspects of turn taking do you think are most important in conversations?
- Why?
- What difficulties may second or foreign language students have with taking turns in a second or foreign language?
- What role does culture play in taking turns for second or foreign language learners?

Of course, different cultures have different notions about what a turn means; for example, in Australia, Aboriginal people can overlap in conversations and take turns whenever they like. This is fine within that culture, but problems can arise in second and foreign language classrooms when the home language, with all its turn-taking conventions, clashes with the language of the school system and all its conventions about how to take turns—resulting, in many cases, in misunderstandings about student behavior (Farrell, 2004b). For example, if a culture permits shouting out a turn at will, and that person enters a second or foreign language classroom that has specific rules for allowing turns, the teacher can misunderstand that the student is disruptive. This is especially true in countries where conversations are steady and a period of silence between a turn is not usual; however, students from cultural backgrounds that have no gaps between turns may not be able to endure these periods of silence unless they have been specifically instructed in turn-taking strategies that emphasize these differences in conversation conventions. For example, when people speak English, they must follow many conventions in face-to-face communications (that go far beyond mere translation from the speaker's mother tongue to English) in order to be fully understood.

People who speak English use a number of strategies (that can be taught) when managing a conversation: when taking a turn, holding a turn, and giving up a turn (Richards, 1990). For example, when we want to take a turn, we can verbally request, physically gesture, or use other such cues. When we want to hold a turn, we can list a sequence and not let others participate until we have finished our list. And when we want to give up our turn, we can simply pause, thus letting another participant take over the turn. These are by no means exhaustive strategies for turn taking, but they will give teachers ideas about how to teach their students the norms of turn taking in the culture of the second or foreign language.

Exploratory Break 6.4
Teaching Turn Taking

In the culture of the second or foreign language you are teaching your students to speak, record a television discussion program (talk show, news broadcast, or game show) and have your students analyze how the different participants do the following:

Take turns

Hold turns

Relinquish turns

Next, role-play such shows and have your students practice these aspects of turn taking.

Topics

An interesting aspect of conversations is how topics are decided. For example, topics have to be introduced by a participant, but not all topics may be appropriate to the given participants, context, and culture.

Exploratory Break 6.5
Establishing Topics

- How do people in a conversation choose a topic to talk about?
- Who decides when a topic can be changed in a conversation?
- What difficulties may second or foreign language students have with establishing topics in a second or foreign language?
- What role does culture play in establishing topics for second or foreign language learners?

For second or foreign language learners who come from a culture where the topic is established by those who have greater age, socioeconomic position, and other such factors, learning that not many of those cultural rules apply in conversations in English in the U.S. can be quite a shock. For example, when most of the English-speaking participants in the U.S. agree on the topic, a participant can usually change it at any time during the conversation and does not need to get permission from other participants regardless of social position or age. Establishing, changing, and/or following the flow of a topic or topics during a conversation, however, can be problematic for second and foreign language learners because it is vitally important for participants to be able to follow the flow of any one topic (Richards, 1990).

Exploratory Break 6.6
Topics

In the culture of the second or foreign language you are teaching your students to speak, record a television discussion program (talk show, news broadcast, or game show) and have your students analyze how the different participants do the following:

Choose topics

Change topics

Follow the flow of topics

> Next, role-play such shows and have your students practice these aspects of the different roles of topics.

Repair

When something happens in a conversation, such as a negotiation between two people, that causes a breakdown in understanding, one or both (or more) participants need to make efforts to correct it.

Exploratory Break 6.7
Conversation Breakdowns

- What can people do when a conversation breaks down?
- What difficulties may second or foreign language students have when trying to repair conversations in a second or foreign language?
- What role does culture play in conversation repair for second or foreign language learners?

In English language, there are some repair strategies that can be incorporated once a conversation has broken down. Of course, the easiest one is to quit the conversation. However, many times, we may not be able to do this and so we may have to employ *self-initiated repair* or seek *other-initiated repair* in order to be able to continue the conversation (Schegloff, Jefferson, & Sacks, 1977). These two strategies may be useful for second or foreign language learners to be aware of when speaking because they can take action to repair or fix their part of the breakdown, called self-initiated repair. For example, when a person is speaking but is not understood, he or she can initiate a repair by saying something like, "What I mean is . . ." or "Let me explain this another way." However, when the repair is initiated by a speaker other than the one who spoke the sentence that was not understood, this is called other-initiated repair. For example, the other participant can say, "Sorry, but I did not understand what you said," or "Can you explain this again?" or "Did you mean . . . ?" So, either the speaker can attempt such repair or the listener can initiate such repair by requesting a clarification.

Exploratory Break 6.8
Repair

In the culture of the second or foreign language you are teaching your students to speak, record a television discussion program (talk show, news broadcast, or game show), and have your students analyze how the different participants make repairs.

- How many times were repairs necessary?
- What method of repairs did the speaker make?
- What method of repairs did the listener make?

Next, role-play such shows and have your students practice these aspects of the different types of repairs in conversations.

Many times, teachers of second and foreign languages forget that there is more to teaching their students to speak in the language beyond teaching the words necessary for going to the bank or the post office (both of which are important functions in the daily lives of their students). Teachers can look at their own daily conversations in the staff room, classrooms, faculty meetings, and home and see how they approach important aspects of speaking in their daily lives. They can document the strategies they use to be successful speakers of English and then teach these strategies to their students so that they can go beyond basic survival to become fully functioning members of the school community and beyond.

Exploratory Break 6.9
Teaching Dimensions of Speaking

- Now that we have discussed three dimensions of conversations, namely, turn taking, choosing topics, and repairing conversations, see if can you come up with innovative ways of teaching awareness of these dimensions to students of English as a second or foreign language.

One way would be to get them to look at conversations in the community; record these conversations (audio and/or video) and bring these recordings to class for all to analyze. The students can role-play these as a group in class.

Accuracy and Fluency

Two further aspects of speaking that have to be taken into account when participating in conversations is the extent to which you want your students speaking accurately and fluently.

Exploratory Break 6.10
Accuracy Versus Fluency

- What does the concept *accuracy* mean to you?
- What does the concept *fluency* mean to you?
- Which aspect of speaking should be most encouraged when speaking a second or foreign language, accuracy or fluency?

An important issue teachers of second and foreign languages must consider is whether you want your language students to speak grammatically correctly all the time (with few errors), or to be more fluent but with some grammatical errors? It seems like an easy question because even native speakers of a language make errors, so some teachers may say, so what? if their students make similar errors. I suggest that language teachers promote both types of practice for their students; however, students may have their own opinions about what they think is important for their needs depending on what type of situation they find themselves in. So I suggest that language teachers inform their students about both approaches. One way of thinking about both accuracy and fluency is to consider that accuracy is a component of fluency rather than an independent part of speaking (Richards, 1990). In this way, second and foreign language teachers can cover both. Additionally, students from different cultural backgrounds may perceive that correct grammar should be used at all times and thus may not be comfortable making errors (if they notice them). Teachers may have to reassure them that errors are a natural part of speech even for native speakers. One way of doing this is to watch TV programs (see Chapter 8 on listening for a detailed method of using TV "soaps" for listening and speaking practice) and TV debates to see how many errors people make as they speak.

DIAGNOSING ESL STUDENTS' SPOKEN ENGLISH

Before we get into the actual teaching of the speaking skill, it is important to be able to diagnose our students' spoken English. Although I give details about oral testing in Chapter 9, "Language Assessment," I want to give you some idea about how you can look at "problems" your learners may have with speech. So, I suggest you collect all the information you can about your students' speech (and writing, listening, and reading) by interviewing them about when they usually speak English outside the class and also by recording them (with their permission) while they speak in class. This way, you can identify which learners have specific problems speaking and which problems are common for all your learners. When diagnosing your students' general spoken English ability, Herbert (2002, pp. 190–191) suggests we look at the following suprasegmental levels:

- Clarity: Is the learner's speech clear?
- Speed: Does the learner speak too quickly?
- Loudness: Does the learner speak too softly?
- Breathing: Does the learner speak with appropriate pauses, breathing each utterance into groups?
- Fluency: Does the learner speak with either long silences between words or too many "filled pauses" (e.g., "ah, ummm")?
- Voice: Is there enough variation in pitch?
- Eye gaze: Does the learner use eye-gaze behavior appropriate to the context (e.g., facing a conversational partner or looking at the audience if delivering an oral presentation)?
- Expressive behavior: Does the learner overuse gestures? Does the facial expression match the utterance?

After looking at your data about the class and individual students' spoken English ability, it may be easier for you to choose and design activities for your speaking lessons, because now you have more information about what needs to be practiced and what you can realistically achieve given the students you have. In other words, you can prioritize your activities based on what you think your students need.

GUIDELINES FOR PREPARING SPEAKING LESSONS

When preparing lessons for a speaking class, it is important to consider the following four guidelines:

1. *Activities should have a preactivity and a postactivity component.* For preactivities, students can be introduced to the topic and given the necessary information about the situation they are about to study. If necessary, and depending on their proficiency levels, students can be given vocabulary that may be helpful for them for that particular activity. Students can

brainstorm setting up the task, simulation, or role-play. It is important to remember that when setting up a role-play, the teacher must decide if the students will prepare all the language they will use in the role-play (controlled role-play), prepare part of the language (enough to scaffold them through the opening of the role-play), or just let the language develop naturally as the role-play develops. If group work is involved (see below for more details), then one reporter can make a postactivity report (as in a problem-solving activity) or the whole group can perform the role-play.

2. *Activities should encourage as many students as possible to speak.* If teachers call on individual students, students will have limited opportunities to speak because the teacher is controlling which students and how often they participate in class. However, if teachers set up activities in which pair work and group work is encouraged, this stimulates greater class participation by everyone in the class. Yes, some teachers may worry that pair work or group work can be noisy, that it allows lazy students to stay silent, and that not all the proficiency levels of students can be matched. While all these criticisms are valid, I suggest that the advantages in terms of participation and opportunity to practice speaking are much greater. In fact, second language acquisition research has recently suggested that activities and tasks that encourage a negotiation of meaning can lead to higher levels of second language proficiency (Pica, Young, & Doughty, 1987). A combination of pair work and group work is called a *pyramid discussion* (Jordan, 1990). To organize discussion as a pyramid discussion, first give a problem to pairs of students to solve. After the problem has been solved, two more pairs come together to compare answers and to agree to a group answer (there are four students together at this time). This combining of groups of four continues in a pyramid style until the whole class is finally together agreeing on one class answer.

3. *If using pair work and/or group work, activities should be timed and each participant in the group should have an assigned role.* If, for example, you have four group members in each group, then assign the following roles: group leader—this person makes sure all members participate and that the task is completed; group scribe—this person writes the group (not his or her own) opinion; group timekeeper—this person keeps the group informed about time issues related to the task; and group reporter—this person will report the group's (and not his or her own opinion) result to the class.

4. *Activities should have observable outcomes.* Speaking for speaking's sake is fine, but when teaching speaking to second or foreign language learners, students should have a clear idea of what is required from the activity. One way of ensuring this is to have a clearly required outcome for each activity. For example, students may be required to rank a list into

some order, which suggests that a pair or group must agree to the ranking. They can also be required to match similarities, distinguish differences, solve problems, list causes or effects, or produce something such as specific materials, a play, a book, and so forth.

Exploratory Break 6.11
Guidelines for Planning Speaking Lessons

- What activities can you think of that would be suitable for speaking activities in the preactivity phase of the class? Postactivity phase of the class?
- Design a pyramid-style problem-solving activity that gets the class as a whole to finally arrive at a class solution (see previous section).
- What observable outcomes would be suitable for speaking activities?

A STRATEGIC APPROACH TO TEACHING SPEAKING

I have used the following class project (adapted from Helgesen, Brown, & Mandeville, 1987) for many years with second and foreign language students, regardless of their proficiency levels, to promote speaking skills (and all other skills, too). The class project activity also follows the guidelines set out previously by having students work individually, in pairs, and in groups where they must negotiate meaning and solve problems in order to arrive at an end product while all the time speaking the target language, English. The results of the group project (and this includes each phase of the project as set out below) can be put into a student portfolio (see Chapter 9 on language assessment for more details of portfolio assessment) as evidence of student work.

In order to begin this activity, it is best for students to form groups. Based on my experience with this activity, groups of four should be the maximum amount, as any more group members can lead to such problems as one or more members not doing similar amounts of work, one or more members doing all the work, or one or more members having no defined role within the group. When the groups have been decided, each group must address the following issues:

Project focus

Project purpose

Project information

Project tasks

Project report

Project focus

In order to address the issue of project focus, students must first discuss project ideas. Of course, the beauty of this question is that it allows subject teachers and immersion teachers to incorporate their curriculum while at the same time promoting language proficiency. For example, teachers of history can use this activity for native as well as nonnative speakers by assigning a history project that covers the curriculum. However, if teachers want to allow their students to decide their own project focus, then this can be accomplished by brainstorming various topics and then deciding on one topic that all agree on. For example, some Korean students of mine decided on the following topics in a brainstorming session: pen pals, student lifestyles, bike tours, city tours, and internationalization of Korean food. Then, after discussion, the group decided on internationalization of Korean food as their project. Of course, during the discussions, students will practice all aspects of spoken conversations covered in this chapter, such as topic selection and change, turn taking, and conversation repair (self-initiated and other-initiated). Teachers may want to monitor these conversations to see how successfully they have incorporated these. Teachers will also have to monitor levels of fluency versus accuracy. I suggest that fluency takes precedence here and, if the teacher is concerned about errors, he or she can monitor and take note of the most common grammatical errors he or she hears without interrupting the flow of the group's conversation. Later, the teacher can go over these errors in a feedback session so that they are not fossilized.

Exploratory Break 6.12
Project Focus

- Can you think of any other methods (besides brainstorming) of deciding a project focus? (For example, the Internet may be a useful source.)

Project Purpose

When they have decided on the topic, they can then write a brief description of the project and its purpose. I think it best that the group be asked to produce a written result of this phase of the project both for the teacher's record and for the group's records. For example, the Korean students wrote the following (in its original English):

> We have been watching many foreigners who had problems talking about Korean food. So, that gave us a great motivation to do this project. We will modify the Korean food to be agreeable to them while conserving our traditional taste in it. We will create a new Korean food that we will call "International."

However, before the group writes anything on paper, they should be encouraged to discuss the purpose first. Additionally, it may be an interesting idea to have each group report their purpose to the class so all will be aware of the purpose of each project.

Project Information

Each group must decide where they can get the necessary information to be able to complete their project. For example, the Korean group decided to get information from surveys of people, reading cookbooks and magazines, and watching cooking shows on the television. In this Internet age, students have a huge resource center at their fingertips; however, teachers may want to monitor their use of the Internet as not all sources are valid. I suggest that teachers build a library component into this phase of the project so that students can get practice using this as a source for research.

Exploratory Break 6.13
Project Information

- Can you think of any other sources that students can use to get information for a project (e.g., databases, books, experts, etc.)?

Project Tasks

Each group must next decide on specific items that need to be completed and devise a schedule for this. For example, the Korean group decided to break up the research on food for each of the four group members: one member taking grains, one vegetables, one meats, and the other beverages. This would be accomplished in four weeks. Next, they would come together and compare what they found and then develop a "new" taste in the following two weeks. So it is important that the teacher shows the students how to make a matrix of schedules and to make sure that each group remains on track by asking for frequent updates. These updates can be given in spoken form during class so that they not only practice speaking but also inform both the teacher and the other groups about the project's progress. This also motivates each group participant to take responsibility to complete whatever task was assigned in a timely manner.

Project Report

The final phase of this project activity entails deciding how the group will make its final report to the class and the teacher. I usually require both an oral and written report. For the oral report, pairs and groups should share the amount of time they spend reporting to the class. The oral report can be accompanied by a video report (as the Korean "international food" group did), and/or a role-play, but it all depends on the topic of the project. Both the teacher and the other students in the class can provide feedback. The feedback and assessment can also be negotiated by the class before the start of the project so that each student knows what is expected. Of course, with modern technology, the report can now be put on a CD and a copy distributed to each member of the class.

Exploratory Break 6.14
Class Project

Following the explanations above about how to set up a class project, decide on the following:

- What will the project be about?
- What is the purpose of the project?
- Where can you get information about the project?
- How will you schedule particular tasks?
- How will you report the results of the project?

CHAPTER REFLECTION

Speaking a second or foreign language can be an anxiety-provoking activity for even the bravest of people. This is because the speaker must not only think in the second or foreign language but also produce the second or foreign language—and all this in a very narrow time span. However, teachers of second and foreign languages can help their students better master the art of speaking if they make them more aware of the strategies they can employ during conversations to comprehend better and be better understood. A class project can be a wonderful activity to get students in any class, subject matter, immersion, and/or ESL or EFL class to practice many of these speaking strategies, not to mention all the other skill areas.

CHAPTER SEVEN

Teaching Reading

People read for many different reasons; two of the most important are for pleasure and for information. People read many different types of books, magazines, journals, and newspapers. Some people like fiction, others like to read romantic pieces, and still others like to read history. People also read in different ways and at different times of the day and night. For example, I like to read academic material early in the morning but not in the evening, and I like to read novels in the evening or at night. It is important for teachers of English language to be aware of their own reading habits, what they like and dislike to read and how they like to read (the strategies they use), before they attempt to teach others how to read. This awareness can lead teachers to become more sensitive to their students' learning needs, especially those of English as a second or foreign language learners.

Exploratory Break 7.1
Reading Habits

- What genre of reading material do you like to read best (romance, horror, fiction, history, etc.)? Why?
- What genre do you not like to read? Why?
- When do you like to read for pleasure?
- When do you like to read for information?

What did you discover about your reading habits? What did you discover about how you like to read? Do you, for example, like to underline important points in a text? Do you like to reread or not? Do you like to write a summary? These are all strategies that have been identified that "good" readers supposedly use. If you become more aware of the strategies you, as a successful reader (you would not be reading this book if you were not a successful reader), use, you can have a better perspective on teaching reading to students who are more challenged with this skill and who, for the most part, see reading as an uninteresting and painful process. This chapter gives English language teachers in their first years a general introduction to the reading process and what it means to teach reading strategies. The chapter outlines various activities and exercises second and foreign language and immersion teachers can use when teaching reading strategies (useful strategies used by fluent readers) to their students. The strategies covered include activating prior knowledge, prediction, skimming, scanning, teaching vocabulary, and recognizing text structure. You can compare these strategies with the ones you like to use to provide a strategic approach to teaching reading.

READING

This section will give you some background about what readers actually do when they have to read. Look at Exploratory Break 7.2 first to start reflecting about the reading process.

Exploratory Break 7.2
Reading Definition

- Define what reading is.
- Explain the reading process as best you can.
- Do readers (first and second language users) use their previous knowledge and experience of the topic when trying to understand the meaning of a passage?
- Do readers depend on the text itself for information on a topic?

If we take reading at its most basic physical act, we can say that the act of reading, as Aebersold and Field (1997, p. 15) suggest, "is what happens when people look at a text and assign meaning to the written symbols in that text." It is the interaction between the text and the reader that creates meaning. Models of reading in a first language have been created to describe this interaction between reader and text, and what happens when people read. The three main models of how reading occurs are bottom-up theory, top-down theory, and interactive theory. These models have also been used to describe how reading in a second or foreign language occurs.

I will outline these three main theories (or models) for explaining the reading process. Interestingly enough, these three models can also be used when trying to understand the listening process (see Chapter 8), so please take note when you are reading the next chapter on listening. One model of reading, called the top-down model, argues that readers bring prior knowledge and experiences to the text and that they continue to read as long as the text confirms their expectations. This top-down process can be explained as follows: Readers first look at a passage or a text. Then they guess or predict what the text will be about (based on their prior knowledge and experience of the topic) after reading the title, headings, and subheadings. The readers then continue to read the text, seeking confirmation about the topic based on their prior knowledge of that topic. So readers fit the text into knowledge and experiences they already hold.

A second model of how reading occurs, called the bottom-up model, suggests that a reader reads the words and sentences and looks at the organization of the text (without relating it to experience or prior knowledge) in order to construct meaning from what was written in the text—meaning that depends on knowledge of both vocabulary and syntax. The bottom-up process can be explained as follows: When we read, one thing we do is extract the propositions from the text. How? By chunking the sentences into constituents and constructing the propositions from there. Comprehension then depends on the propositions we have extracted that serve as the basis of what we understand and recall (J. C. Richards, personal communication, 2002). This is the opposite of the top-down approach; instead of working from meaning to text (top-down), this model has a reader working from text to meaning (with a focus at the word and sentence level).

A third model of how reading works, called the interactive model (Stanovich, 1980), argues that both top-down and bottom-up processes occur when a person reads a text.

Exploratory Break 7.3
Models of Reading

- Which of the three models used to explain the reading process do you subscribe to and why?

  Top-down model

  Bottom-up model

  Interactive model

- Do you have a different model that may better explain the reading process to you?

Let us now define reading. For me, one of the best definitions of reading that I have seen is from Anthony, Pearson, and Raphael (1993):

> Reading is the process of constructing meaning through the *dynamic interaction* among the reader's existing knowledge, the information suggested by the written language, and the context of the reading situation. (p. 284)

It really sums up all of what I have presented so far in this chapter about the reading process: the reading process involves the reader in active interaction with what is presented in the text. The reader brings important past experiences to the text and encodes the meaning of the text based on his or her prior experiences.

GUIDELINES FOR PREPARING READING LESSONS

Teachers of reading are urged to remember the following points when preparing effective second or foreign language reading lessons (from Farrell, 2002):

• *Activate prior knowledge.* As in teaching listening lessons, we must remember that the student reader himself or herself brings something important to the text—previously acquired schemata. These schemata are networks of prior interpretations and they become the basis for comprehension. The text is filtered through these pre-existing schemata and the reader will try to match these pre-existing schemata with what he or she reads in the text. Remember, the student readers themselves, rather than the writer, construct the meaning of the text. Readers actively try to make connections between the text and what they already know about the world based on their cultural values, native language, and discourse processes.

• *Build in activities that have students practice all reading processes.* The process of reading comprehension is a combination of top-down and bottom-up processes, not just one of them. So, when the reader tries to comprehend, there is a "bouncing back-and-forth" between the reader and the text, between a reader's top-down knowledge of the topic and the text. Comprehension is then reached (hopefully). If it is not, readers will make readjustments until comprehension is reached. This is why we must teach ESL or EFL, immersion, and reluctant native speaker readers specific strategies they can use to help them comprehend a text. The teacher of reading should provide training in both the top-down and bottom-up processes. Some reading activities are top-down (e.g., prediction), some are bottom-up (e.g., vocabulary), and some are both (e.g., text structure). However, if the students are seen as stronger in one area, then compensatory instruction may need to be directed to the deficit area.

• *Provide students with interesting reading topics.* As teachers and adults, we typically will not read material on topics in which we are not interested, so why should we ask our students to read topics in which they have no interest? Try to survey your students' levels of interest in different genres (horror, science fiction, romance, etc.) and look for material they can read with interest. Of course, it would be impossible to cater to all students in one class unless you bring in an extensive reading program to your reading classes. You can start a class library for this. Ask students to bring in their favorite book and then have them share it with the class. Or, if you have funds, get the students to make a list of interesting reading material and start a reading library in your class.

Exploratory Break 7.4
Reading Strategy Profile

Make a reading strategy profile (using the previous guidelines) for each student in your class (you already did a similar exercise for yourself in Exploratory Break 7.1). Make a plan for each student for the coming semester by considering the following questions:

• Which strategies do your students excel at?
• Which strategies do your students need to work on?
• How do you propose to help or encourage each student to develop her or his strategic reading skills?
• How do you plan to monitor your students' progress in attaining specific reading strategies?
• How can you motivate your students to take a strategic approach to reading the English language?

A STRATEGIC APPROACH TO TEACHING READING

Generally, strategy research tells us that all students use various strategies when they read, even if these strategies are completely ineffective. In fact, I really think that no strategy is "good" or "bad" because what works for one reader may not necessarily work for another reader. For example, I do not like to use a highlighter on my text to mark important ideas when I am reading; rather, I like to take notes or write on the text itself. However, a major problem less-skilled readers have while reading is that they do not often engage in comprehension monitoring. That is, they do not notice that they do not understand what they are reading—that the reading process is breaking down—and thus they feel frustrated when they attempt to read. Consequently, these less-skilled readers should be taught a more strategic approach to learning how to read.

Exploratory Break 7.5
Reading Strategies

Explain what each of the following strategies are and then compare your answer with what you read below:

- Prior knowledge
- Prediction
- Skimming
- Scanning
- Vocabulary
- Text structure

While you raise the level of your students' awareness about these reading strategies, you may want to check their attitudes about reading. You may want to note which students talk positively about the reading material, who uses the language creatively, and who shows interest in reading as a result of reading strategically.

PRIOR KNOWLEDGE

Schema theory suggests that readers have prior knowledge about a topic before they read. This prior knowledge can be similar to (and thus elaborated on) what the reader will encounter in a new text. Alternatively, it may be in conflict with the topic or nonexistent. In these cases, teachers can play a vital role in seeing that the readers' knowledge about the new topic is built up so that they can successfully comprehend a new text. The following three activities can help reading teachers activate the relevant background schema of their students (from Farrell, 2000). Remember also that this and other strategies can be used to teach listening comprehension (see the next chapter).

Exploratory Break 7.6
Prior Knowledge

- Can you think of ways you can get your students to think about a topic before they read a text?
- Compare your answer to the activities outlined below.

Now I offer you three specific methods of activating your students' prior knowledge about a topic before they read a text: *word association, direct experience,* and *cinquain.*

Word Association

The rationale behind the word association task is to determine what prior knowledge students bring to a new topic before they have read the text. It works as follows: Students respond (orally at first) to a key word or phrase such as "sport is useful." Next, the students write down as many words or phrases as possible in three minutes that relate to this key phrase (e.g., sport is useful: healthy, expensive, fun, hard work, lose weight). The teacher then writes these words on the board. Alternatively, the students can be asked to free write on the topic. For this activity, students write everything about the topic for five minutes. While they are writing, the students should not worry about their grammar, spelling, or punctuation. The emphasis at this stage is on content, not accuracy. The teachers can use the knowledge they get about their students' knowledge of the topic for their lesson planning.

Exploratory Break 7.7
Word Association

- Can you think of any other activities (e.g., using concept maps) that you can adapt for a word association task?

Direct Experience (Hands-on Learning)

For this method, the students are required to get up from their seats and participate directly in some activity (such as sport). The rationale behind the direct experience, or hands-on learning, is that students build on their background knowledge through firsthand experiences with concepts and vocabulary important to the lesson. Of course, the teacher must indicate which words or concepts are going to be important and write these on the board. This method requires the teacher to take the students through several steps and introduce a sport that may incite curiosity in the students. The following steps should be observed for this process, and the teacher should ensure the students go through the steps in the order they appear below:

Step 1: Identify concepts important to the lesson.

Step 2: Identify vocabulary that names those concepts.

Step 3: Prepare a lesson that requires the students to directly participate in an activity that develops the concepts and uses the vocabulary.

Exploratory Break 7.8
Direct Experience

- Can you think of any activities or examples that you can use for direct experience or hands-on learning (e.g., see the example on taekwondo that follows)?
- My example answer for taekwondo (a Korean martial art) is as follows:

Concepts: self-development, character development, equality.

Vocabulary: excellence, pride, satisfaction, peak, instill, discipline, determination, open, neighborhood, enjoyment.

New sport: taekwondo. All students should stand up and stretch their arms and legs (this works especially well in afternoon classes). They then sit and stretch. The students are then taken through various exercise routines that are associated with taekwondo. Thus, students get firsthand experience in a sport they are not likely to have experienced before. This also keeps attention focused on the lesson.

Cinquain

Another method that reading teachers can use to activate background knowledge is having the students write a cinquain. A cinquain is a five-line poem that reflects affective and cognitive responses to a concept. The rationale behind the cinquain is that it helps students develop prior knowledge for subsequent lessons in a poetic fashion. However, not many students will have experienced such a style of writing. Also, it is a challenging and creative activity. The following steps should be observed, and the teacher should ensure the students go through them in the order they appear below:

Line 1: One word title

Line 2: Two words that describe the title

Line 3: Three words expressing an action

Line 4: Four words expressing a feeling

Line 5: Another word for the title

Exploratory Break 7.9
Cinquain

Write your own cinquain for the topic of sport. Compare your answer with the one below.

- My example cinquain for the topic of sport is as follows:

Sport

Fun time

Running, jumping, sliding

Laughing, shouting, crying, alive

Living

PREDICTION

Prediction is linked to the strategy of activating prior knowledge. Prediction creates anticipation and gets students thinking about previous experiences they may have had about the topic before they read about it. Research has shown that good readers use prediction as they continue to read a story by seeking to confirm or adjust earlier-made intuitions about the topic. So, prediction works before and while reading. Prediction asks students to guess what will happen next in the story (from chapter headings and subheadings). Prediction involves the readers in active interaction with the text by making them think about what they have read and what they will read next.

Prediction is a strategy used throughout the reading process (pre-, during, and postreading). The procedure includes using the cover of the book, chapter headings, past knowledge, and the text. Prereading activities include having the students guess what will come up in the lesson based on their prior experiences with the topic. During-reading prediction procedures have the students use the text itself and any pictures or illustrations to confirm (or adjust) predictions made during reading. Postreading prediction procedures include having students make adjustments based on their reading of the text. At this post stage, the students confirm (or adjust) predictions made before the reading. In this way, pre-, during-, and postreading activities are linked together to give a coherent understanding of the text.

Exploratory Break 7.10
Prediction

- Develop prediction-type exercises or activities for the following passage:

Running is not a new sport. People were doing it hundreds of years ago. These days, many people run or jog each day as part of their exercise routine. However, some people run in races as their profession. These athletes have to be in very good shape physically in order to run these races. Runners know a good diet is important for their training. They try to eat healthy foods, especially before a race. Every year, there are many long races in many parts of the world. One of the most famous of these races is held in Boston in the United States of America. The Boston race is called the Boston Marathon. This is one of the oldest races in the United States. In 1985, more than 6,000 people ran in the Boston Marathon. They came from all over the world. In some races, the winners get large amounts of money. But for almost a hundred years, they got no money at all in the Boston Marathon. It is only recently that the winners were awarded prize money.

SKIMMING

Skimming is a reading strategy that involves students looking through the text rapidly for the general meaning of an article. Skimming means getting the main point or gist before one reads for detail. Skimming is not an easy reading strategy to teach. This is because skimming assumes that readers (a) have some knowledge of how the text is organized, (b) can notice the main point of a paragraph, and (c) have the ability to infer the main idea of a passage. True/false–type questions on a text can prepare readers for the strategy of skimming. However, teachers should enforce a time limit on the skimming and have the students answer true/false–type questions within the time limit. The objective of skimming is not only to get the gist (main idea) of a passage but also to increase the speed of reading.

Exploratory Break 7.11
Skimming

- Skim through the article in Exploratory Break 7.10 and answer the questions below about the article. Try to put a time limit of one or two minutes on your skimming and answering of questions.

  1. Running is a new sport.   True/False

  2. Some people run in races as a profession.   True/False

  3. Runners have to follow a healthy diet.   True/False

  4. The Boston Marathon is a new race in the U.S.   True/False

  5. Runners come from all over to run in the Boston Marathon.
     True/False

SCANNING

Scanning is a reading strategy that involves students reading to find specific information. Students can learn that they do not have to read every word in the text to obtain specific information. It is a slower process than skimming. However, this strategy is still a high-speed activity, and teachers should develop questions that involve students looking for exact information in the text in a competitive-type format. This competitive aspect of the strategy used in a classroom is important, as time limits help reinforce the idea that the students should not read every word in a text.

Exploratory Break 7.12
Scanning

- Scan the article again in Exploratory Break 7.10 and this time answer the questions below that seek specific information.

    1. What do many people do as part of their exercise routine these days?

    2. In 1985, how many people ran in the Boston Marathon?

    3. When do the runners eat healthy foods especially?

    4. When were the participants awarded prize money for the first time in the Boston Marathon?

TEACHING NEW VOCABULARY

Sometimes students may need to guess the meaning of a word they do not know while reading a text because they have no dictionary or they are in an examination-type situation. Reading teachers can teach the relationships between words in a text by using strategies such as the following:

- Contrast: The word means the opposite of another word or expression in the text. Example: A frugal boss will never give a generous bonus at the end of the year. [frugal: generous]
- Cause: The word is the cause of something described in the text. Example: Anorexia is a disease attributed to many deaths in young girls because they want to lose too much weight. [anorexia: lose too much weight = death]
- Consequence: The word is used to describe the result of something. Example: Lung cancer can result from too much smoking. [smoking: cancer]
- Explanation: The meaning of the word is explained, a definition is given, or an example is given. Example: Kimchee, a Korean fermented cabbage, is a delicious food. [Kimchee: fermented cabbage]
- Hyponyms. A reader may be able to see the relationship between a familiar and unfamiliar word by looking at the general word class, such as boat, ship, tanker, and supertanker, where boat is used as a

hyponym. Example: We must prevent oil spills from supertankers. An example took place in 1970 near Spain when an oil spill from a wrecked tanker exploded into fire. These types of ships are difficult to control in busy waters. [supertanker: tanker: ship]

- Definition. Definitions of words may sometimes be found in the text. Example: Neuralgia, a sharp, violent pain along a nerve pathway, can be treated with aspirin. [neuralgia: nerve pain]
- Punctuation. Readers can use the punctuation in the sentence to figure out the meaning of the word they do not know. For example, readers can use such clues as italics (showing how a word is defined), quotation marks (showing the word has special meaning), dashes (showing apposition, definitions), and/or brackets (enclosing a definition). Example: Taekwondo—a Korean martial art—is very good for self-defense. [meaning between two dashes]
- Inference. Contexts give examples from which a reader can infer the meaning of a term. Example: The misogynist manager disliked all the women in his office, so they all resigned. [misogynist: woman hater]

Exploratory Break 7.13
Teaching New Vocabulary

- Develop some exercises (you could use the topic of sport) that help students guess the meaning of words from the context for each of the outlined strategies.
  For example, which example of using contextual cues does the following sentence practice: Taekwondo—a Korean martial art—is very good for developing flexibility. [punctuation]
- Alternatively, try to find an authentic text (from a newspaper or a magazine) that uses some of the above examples.

One method of checking students' knowledge of vocabulary before a lesson is using a semantic web. This vocabulary-building strategy gives students access to what they already know about a topic or word. Students think of words related to the topic of the text and then organize these words into meaningful associations. See the taekwondo example in Figure 7.1, and then make your own semantic web about the teaching of reading and compare it with a partner's.

Figure 7.1

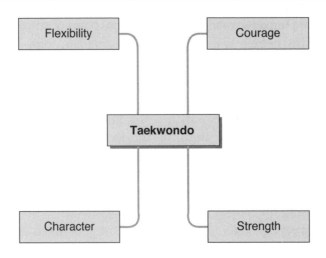

TEACHING TEXT STRUCTURE

Grabe (2002, p. 279) has suggested that teaching students awareness of text structure is important for their comprehension because, as he reminds us, "learners who are aware of text structure have better comprehension abilities." One aspect of text structure we can inform our students about is that writers generally write their texts in such a way that more important ideas are highlighted. Also, it is important to remember that knowledge of how texts are structured can be transferred to writing. So, if our students are taught how texts are structured, they may be able to do the following:

- Distinguish between main ideas and supporting details
- Identify main ideas
- Write summaries
- Understand how parts of the text are related and recognize cohesive devices that writers use
- Use this knowledge to write more clearly

So, how are texts structured? Four main types have been identified among academic texts that English language students will be most involved with: collection/description, cause and effect, problem and solution, and comparison.

Collection/Description

It is the simplest type and one that is used by very young children in storytelling. A subset of collection is description. Under this, we club attributes, specifics, explanations, examples, and additional qualities. It also includes the who, what, where, when, and why structure of journalistic writing.

Example: Our Sports Day was held late last year. It was held in the main sports area of the school. All the teachers and students turned up to see a wide variety of events. The students played soccer, ran many races, and ate lots of food after the sporting events. There were many winners of the vast number of events. We all enjoyed the Sports Day.

The emphasis here is on "played soccer," "ran many races," "ate lots of food," and "there were many winners."

Cause and Effect

Cause and effect is one pattern that often uses signal words in the form of verbs, but these are not easy to spot because they do not stand out in a sentence like other signal words. One way of getting students to recognize cause-and-effect-type texts is by asking questions that have them answer what happens as a result of an action. Teachers can explain the action, such as, "I trained hard every day for six months in preparation for the race." This is a cause statement. The effect, or result, is what happened as a result of the action, such as, "I won the race." Also, cause-and-effect relationships in texts are, for the most part, likely to be single, or one-to-one. Here is another example:

Example: However, not all the star student athletes performed well during the Sports Day. John, for example, wasn't competing well because he had an upset stomach. As a result, he lost every race he entered. His parents and his friends were very disappointed to see this. They all hoped he would perform better the next year.

Cause: Not all the star athletes performed well. John was not competing well.

Effect: John lost every race. His parents and friends were disappointed.

Problem and Solution

Texts that present the reader with a problem usually include a solution or at least a proposed solution to the stated problem. In order to recognize this pattern, students should skim through the text after the problem has been stated and look for key words that outline some of the solutions. These key words can include signal words (unlike causation), such as time or order signals: first, second, third . . .

Example: These days, many soccer experts are asking how referees can do a better job. With so much money involved in the winning and losing of games, some soccer experts are speaking openly of getting rid of some bad referees because they make bad decisions during the game; for instance, they sometimes cannot see a foul on the field of play. One solution is to use video replays for controversial decisions. Another solution would be to hire professional referees.

Problem: Some referees make bad decisions. The referees sometimes cannot see a foul.

Solution: Use video replays. Hire professional referees.

Comparison

When writers want to compare things, they want to explain how they are alike. When they want to contrast things, they want to explain how they are different. See the following example:

Example: Today, many athletes take performance-enhancing substances to help them better compete. Despite evidence that taking drugs is harmful, many in sports claim this is not so. Although taking steroids has been related to liver cancer and heart disease, some athletes believe drug taking may enhance their performance.

One view: Taking steroids is harmful, related to liver cancer.

Opposing view: Steroids may enhance performance.

One interesting activity that can have students schematically represent comparable and contrasting aspects of a passage is the use of a Venn diagram. A Venn diagram consists of two circles that partially overlap. Students fill in similar features in the area that overlaps and contrasting features in the separate areas.

Exploratory Break 7.14
Text Structures

- Locate an article on sport (or any other subject or topic) and develop exercises that practice recognition of text structures.

CHAPTER REFLECTION

The goal of most second and foreign language reading programs is to turn "learning to read" into "reading to learn" (Carrell, 1998). The main idea of this chapter is that strategic approaches to teaching reading for English language students can help them better cope with reading English. Additionally, teachers in their first years can find the activities outlined in this chapter easy to use when they first attempt to teach this complicated skill. As you gain more experience teaching reading, you can modify the activities to suit your students' needs.

CHAPTER EIGHT

Teaching Listening

After spending decades outside in the cold as a neglected skill, listening comprehension has finally been raised to a status of crucial importance in language learning, in both learning a first language and learning a second language (Dunkel, 1991). The importance of listening comprehension for second language learning has been highlighted recently (e.g., Nunan, 2002) because, for many foreign and second language students, mastery of the skill of listening is one of the most difficult barriers to overcome to be able to follow lessons, much less become proficient users of the language. Attempting to comprehend a lesson, language or otherwise, can be a harrowing experience for foreign and second language learners unless they have a sensitive and skilled teacher willing to help them achieve levels of understanding that, at the very least, allow them to follow a lesson but, ultimately, help them become functional members of a community in which they have to survive. This is one reason I left listening as the last skill that I will outline; the other is that many of the activities outlined in previous chapters can be used for teaching listening. This chapter, after outlining what listening is, suggests a strategic approach to teaching listening that uses TV "soaps" to show how different activities can make listening an authentic experience in second and foreign language classrooms.

Exploratory Break 8.1
Listening

- What do you think listening is exactly?
- What are the differences between spoken and written language?
- How do these differences impact listening to spoken language?

- Why do people listen?
- How do people listen?
- What potential problems would a second or foreign language learner have in learning to listen?

LISTENING

What is listening? This seems like an easy question to answer because we take it for granted (unless we are hearing impaired, of course). That said, it is interesting that listening-comprehension researchers in first language studies cannot agree on an exact definition of what it means to listen. For example, Dunkel (1991) cites the existence of 34 different definitions of listening comprehension. However, according to Nunan (2002), two important processes have dominated language listening pedagogy for some time: bottom-up and top-down processing (see previous chapter on reading for a full discussion of these processes, as they have similar implications for understanding the process of listening), in which top-down refers to incoming messages as a source for information, while bottom-up processing occurs when listeners use background knowledge as an aid to understand the incoming message (Nunan, 2002; Richards, 1990). When a learner starts to process an incoming message using a bottom-up approach, he or she listens to sounds, words, and sentences to make sense of the message. For this to happen, the listener must make use of his or her knowledge of how sounds are streamed (phonological awareness), how sentences are organized (grammar cues), and what words are used (vocabulary).

Exploratory Break 8.2
Bottom-Up Processing

- This exploratory break will give you practice developing various activities that practice bottom-up processes.
- Develop a listening activity that requires the students to

distinguish important words in a passage,

recognize verb tense,

identify various parts of speech,

be able to tell if a sentence is active or passive.

In order to help you with Exploratory Break 8.2, you could have them listen to a passage that you have prepared with a specific focus (depending on what you want them to listen for—see previous discussion), and ask them to underline the feature you want, or write it, match it, and so forth. The main point of bottom-up activities is to get the students with lower-proficiency levels to practice listening for particular features of the language. One activity I like to use is to have the students listen to a song and listen for specific words. When listeners use their previous knowledge of a subject to make sense of the message in the form of schema (see Chapter 6 on reading), they are using a top-down approach to listening comprehension.

Exploratory Break 8.3
Top-Down Processing

- This exploratory break will give you practice developing various activities that practice top-down processes. Most activities in top-down processing have students infer the meaning of a passage based on their knowledge of a topic.
- Develop a listening activity that requires the students to

  infer the topic of the passage,

  infer the role of the various participants in a passage,

  listen to the end of a story and guess the beginning,

  guess the ending of a story.

Again, to help you with Exploratory Break 8.3, you could have them listen to a passage that you have prepared with a specific focus (depending on what you want them to listen for—see previous discussion), and ask them to write it (start a story or complete the story), to match the story with pictures, and so forth. Generally, listeners make use of both approaches to understand a message, but if they do not have any previous knowledge of the topic of the incoming message, they will then rely on their knowledge of vocabulary, grammar, and sentences to try to comprehend the incoming message (bottom-up).

LISTENING PURPOSE

Generally, people listen to each other to communicate with each other in conversations. They may just want to listen to what someone else says but not take part, or they may want to take part and interact with the other person. People also listen for information: they listen to the news, the weather, the radio, and the TV for specific information or entertainment. They may also listen to a lecture or someone giving instructions so that they can follow what was suggested. In short, people have different purposes for listening. So, listeners can be said to play different roles, which not only depend on the situation in which they are involved, but also depend on the purpose of the communication.

Richards (1990) makes a distinction between two main purposes of communication, *interactional* and *transactional.* In transactional communication, the main purpose is to exchange information, whereas in interactional communication, it is to maintain social relationships. Rather than suggest that these are the only two purposes for listening, I should point out that the two terms represent a continuum, from communicating for social reasons to communicating for information to complete some transaction. In fact, many interactions fall in between these two extremes; for example, we greet each other more often than not before we get down to business.

INTERACTIONAL LISTENING

When the incoming message is purely for social purposes, such as complimenting or making small talk, this is interactional, as both the speaker and listener are trying to connect socially.

Exploratory Break 8.4
Interactional Purposes

- Developing activities that practice listening for interactional purposes involves getting the students to identify general aspects of interactional language such as small talk, jokes, compliments, and so forth.
- Develop listening activities that have your students

  identify specific differences in language used for interaction and for transaction,

  identify compliments,

  identify jokes,

  identify small talk.

TRANSACTIONAL LISTENING

On the other hand, messages may be conveyed in order to transfer information of some sort; this is a transactional use of language between speaker and listener. Whereas interactional listening is listener oriented, transactional listening is message oriented (Richards, 1990).

Exploratory Break 8.5
Transactional Purposes

- Developing activities that practice listening for transactional purposes involve getting the students to identify specific transactional purposes such as to carry out specific tasks or identify a sequence of events or activities.
- Develop listening activities that have your students listen to

  follow instructions for assembling a table;

  write down exactly what was said, such as to follow instructions in a message;

  write down train times;

  summarize a lecture.

Richards (1990) has further developed listening purposes into a four-part classification that includes all four aspects of listening discussed thus far—interactional, transactional, top-down, and bottom-up—into one framework for comparing the different demands of listening. For example, some activities in listening call for a combination of interactional and bottom-up (telling a story to someone for fun), interactional and top-down (listening to talk at a cocktail party where people follow certain rituals of introductions but do not engage in important talk [Richards, 1990]), transactional and bottom-up (learning something for the first time—cooking—and thus using bottom-up processing), and transactional and top-down (using prior knowledge of a topic and thus using top-down processing to confirm comprehension of the incoming message).

INTERACTIVE LISTENING

Interactive listening can also take place in all four aspects of listening: interactional, transactional, bottom-up, or top-down. In interactive listening, the listener must be able to display signs of collaboration and understanding to fulfill his role as a participant in a conversation. Rost (1990) identifies 11 strategies that listeners must be able to use in order to be effective in conversation. Among these, I will outline three particular strategies that are of great importance to second and foreign language learners:

1. Back-channel signals to the speaker to signal understanding

2. Use of language to fix nonunderstanding of situations

3. Use of language to check understanding

BACK-CHANNEL SIGNALS

The first type of strategy consists in listeners' provision of appropriate *back-channel signals* to speakers to indicate that they understand the conversation. These signals can be verbal, semiverbal ("mm," "uh huh"), or nonverbal (e.g., nodding). In the example below, the listener in Turn 4 and 6 indicates that he is following his interlocutor by using "mm":

1. W: You've got a TV there then.

2. M: Yes. [pause] I've been trying to get a football game.

3. W: I've been trying mine, too, but I can't get a thing.

4. M: Mm.

5. W: I really need to watch this game.

6. M: Mm.

Schegloff (1981), though, says that back-channel signals "at best claim attention and/or understanding, rather than showing it or evidencing it" (p. 78). To him, their most common usage is to show that the listener understands an extended unit of speech is underway, and that the speaker should continue talking.

Exploratory Break 8.6
Back-Channel Signals

Can you think of any more common back-channel signals that native speakers of English use? List them.

- Record a discussion on TV and transcribe all the back-channel signals used. Do they match your list?
- How would you teach these back-channel signals to second and foreign language students?

LOCAL, GLOBAL, AND TRANSITIONAL REPAIRS

The second type of strategy is used when listeners experience understanding problems in conversations and want to fix them. Rost (1990, 1991) identifies three categories of listener repair: local, global, and transitional. When using a local query, the listener notices a section of the conversation as a problem. In the next example, the listener in Turn 2 repeats the word that he does not understand:

1. A: If you have your application form finished, take it to Room 312.

2. B: Application?

With a global query, the listener indicates an understanding problem with the whole conversation. In the following example, the listener in Turn 2 does not identify any particular item as posing a comprehension problem, but rather asks the speaker to repeat the whole sentence:

1. A: Will you go to the house tonight or tomorrow?

2. B: I don't understand. Can you speak more slowly?

By using a transitional query, the listener indicates he or she has trouble predicting the meaning of specific information. In the next example, the listener in Turn 2 understands what she is asked to do, but needs to verify this.

1. A: Can you take this to the manager, please?

2. B: Is this the branch manager?

Exploratory Break 8.7
Local, Global, and Transitional Repairs

- Can you think of any more common repairs that native speakers of English use? List them.
- Record a discussion on TV and transcribe all the repairs in conversations used. Do they match your list?
- How would you teach these to second and foreign language students?

COMPREHENSION CHECKS

The third type of strategy is in the form of comprehension checks listeners use to make sure they have understood or to clarify unclear information. In the next example, the listener in Turn 3 understands the speaker's utterance but finds it unclear, and must clarify.

1. G: When did you want me to come to your house?

2. T: Oh, any time between now and next Monday.

3. G: You mean a week from today?

4. T: Yeah.

Exploratory Break 8.8
Comprehension Checks

- Can you think of any common comprehension checks that native speakers of English use? List them.
- Record a discussion on TV and transcribe all the comprehension checks used. Do they match your list?
- How would you teach these to second and foreign language students?

Although research on second and foreign language acquisition has stressed the importance of interactive listening strategies, teachers do not seem to be teaching them. Traditional listening comprehension practice in second and foreign language classrooms often consists of teachers reading a passage and asking the students to answer a set of related comprehension questions either orally or in writing (Mendelsohn, 1995). Consequently, what takes place in these classrooms is relatively untypical of everyday life situations (Field, 2000). The following sections of guidelines for planning listening lessons and providing a strategic approach to teaching listening highlight the real and interactive nature of listening.

GUIDELINES FOR PREPARING LISTENING LESSONS

The following guidelines may help you prepare lessons for a listening class.

- *Have definite goals for listening comprehension lessons.* Of course, all lessons should have definite goals, but listening lessons should focus on listening first and foremost, and not deviate too much from that focus. I have seen listening comprehension lessons turn into reading or writing lessons after only 10 minutes of listening. So, a listening lesson should teach listening.

- *Require active listening.* Activities should have students participate in some active way. In other words, students should be required to produce some kind of response, either written or spoken, to make sure they are following.

- *Keep anxiety levels low.* Each lesson needs to be structured in order to reduce anxiety so that the students know what to listen for, where to listen, and how to listen. The problem for students is that unlike other skill areas in English, listening is like air: they cannot see anything, so they are not sure if they are listening correctly. The whole listening lesson can be frustrating for the students if they are not guided by the teacher every step of the way until they can do it by themselves.

- *Activate prior knowledge.* Prior knowledge, or schemata, is seen as essential to the comprehension of a second or foreign language. So, lessons should have a built-in triggering of students' schema of a particular topic for a listening activity.

- *Teach listening before you test it.* Above all (and this applies to *all* the skill chapters in this book), listening (and reading, speaking, grammar, and writing) lessons should teach and not only test. It is no good giving students a tape to listen to and answer the comprehension questions that follow because this is just testing their proficiency. We must first teach them how to listen before we test them.

A STRATEGIC APPROACH TO TEACHING LISTENING

In many English language classes, students are presented with listening activities that are contrived and not realistic—because they are too slow or about a topic of no interest to the students—or made for commercial reasons. Even if the students can understand and complete fill-in-the-blank-style exercises during the class, when they go outside into the community, they complain that they still cannot understand real, everyday spoken English. Many times, speakers who have been trained by reading aloud written language, or using tapes on which language is spoken very slowly, are usually shocked when they hear two native speakers talking to each other. One reason for this is that spontaneous spoken language does not sound at all like written language read aloud, which is what the students are usually presented with in a listening class. Since spontaneous spoken language is made up as the speaker speaks, it is less organized and has less information content. Additionally, when teachers provide tasks for their students in which listening and speaking are totally separated, it encourages a passive view of listening skills from both the teacher and the students. Many of the usual listening comprehension practice–type exercises in many classrooms today do not give learners opportunities to interact with the input and show when there is a comprehension problem, or provide feedback that they have understood the message (see previous discussion on interactive listening). However, as Field (2002, p. 244) has observed, in real-life situations that second language learners find themselves interacting in, "listening to a foreign language is a strategic activity." Consequently, learners should be given opportunities to practice both sets of primary skills, speaking and listening, and to integrate them in conversations. They can also be asked to practice reading and writing, depending on the time available. Thus, in this section, my strategic approach to teaching listening is to encourage students to listen to authentic language by listening interactively to soaps on TV. Soaps, although not as spontaneous as real-life speech, can nevertheless offer a close-enough example of real language as it is used in everyday topics.

WHY TV SOAPS?

TV soaps are useful for improving listening comprehension for the following reasons:

> Students usually come into the classroom with TV soap scripts/ schemata already built in from their own lives. All the teacher has to do is to make certain to activate the students' world knowledge of the soap schemata before launching the first stage (see the next section).

> Classroom listening must prepare students for real or authentic listening situations with language that is, as Field (2002, p. 244) says, "the type of foreign language listening that occurs in a real-life encounter or in response to authentic material," which, he says, "is very different" from that of a text that has been graded for a language learner. Soaps provide examples of authentic language that is real and has not been graded for any particular level. Teachers can adjust input to whatever level they want to teach.

> TV soaps are usually programmed on a sequential basis, with either daily or weekly serials. The continuity of such shows allows the individual student room for self-correction, self-pacing, and an increasing familiarity with the show—characters, setting, and mood.

The goal of any listening program should be learner independence, so that students can move from dependence on classroom instruction to listening with full comprehension in the community. The use of TV soaps gives students the opportunity to continue watching the programs after the class or semester has been completed. Also, a self-directed learner will be able to transfer this method to other programs of interest.

METHOD

Lund's (1990) taxonomy of "real-world listening behaviors" (p. 106) is useful to remember when implementing TV soaps. Lund's taxonomy distinguishes between listener function and listener response. For listener function, Lund suggests the following activities: identification, orientation, main idea comprehension, detail comprehension, and full comprehension. Listener response is used to check that these functions have been performed successfully, and this is achieved by any combination of the following: doing, choosing, transferring, answering, condensing, duplicating, modeling, and conversing. Watching TV soaps incorporates all of Lund's listener-function activities and most of the listener-response activities. It should also be noted that the TV soaps approach follows the concept of listening for comprehension (Ur, 1996), which has three main responses:

1. Listener makes no response

2. Listener makes a short response

3. Listener makes a longer response

Of course, as you gain more experience with this method, you can restructure these activities according to your students' needs and proficiency levels. Figure 8.1 illustrates the main procedures of watching TV soaps.

The procedures for each stage all have pre- and post-suggestions, as does the complete method itself.

Stage 1: Fun

The students are asked to watch a particular TV soap and have fun. No response is required. Many students, especially beginning students, will probably not understand anything. The teacher's job here is to reassure the students that this is normal and to encourage them to continue on to the next stage.

Stage 2: Names and Faces

After all the fun of not understanding in Stage 1, students are asked to listen *only* for the names of the characters on the show. They should write these and try to draw a picture of each person. Additional exercises that can be used in Stage 2 are asking students to do the following:

Figure 8.1   TV Soaps Schematic Representation

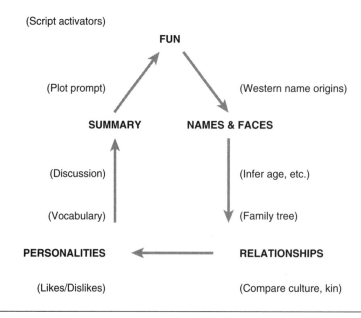

- Identify the setting and socioeconomic status of the people
- Infer each person's age
- Identify the most important person
- Establish who the villains are
- Infer the educational backgrounds of each person
- Identify the amount of familiarity between the characters

Stage 3: Relationships

Now that the students know some of the names of the characters, they now have to establish the relationships between these individuals. Reteaching the necessary family/relations vocabulary will be necessary prior to Stage 3. This is an important stage, not only to reinforce the names recognized in Stage 2, but also because the story will have started to form in the students' subconscious.

Stage 4: Personalities

At this stage, the students should be taught the necessary vocabulary to describe personalities in order to write a personality description of all the characters they have identified and, also, to write about which characters they like and/or dislike.

Stage 5: Summary

By this time, the students should be ready to watch for story content. They will be asked to write a summary of that day's or week's show. This can then be compared to the first stage's frustration of not understanding anything. The students will be surprised at the amount they are actually able to write.

Stage 6: Fun (Again)

The cycle comes full circle and fun returns to watching TV soaps in English. This stage should produce quite a different reaction than that of Stage 1. Even the most basic-level student should have some idea of the general story line, even if this is only one line.

Exploratory Break 8.9
Soap Activities

- I have outlined this six-stage model for listening to soaps. Many more such variations can be incorporated at each stage by any creative teacher.
- Develop some activities for each stage of listening to TV soaps.
- Develop specific interactive listening activities related to the following:

Bottom-up and top-down approaches

Interactional and transactional communication

Back-channel signals

Local, global, and transitional repairs

Comprehension checks

Teachers can often neglect two important aspects of listening when preparing lessons: prelistening activities and postlistening activities (Field, 2002). For prelistening to soaps, students could be prepared for difficult vocabulary and/or grammatical structures they may be faced with. Students can be prepared in the following ways: brainstorming, discussions, prediction exercises, and visual support such as photographs, illustrations, and the like. Preparation of students for this approach entails a triggering of their schemata, or script, for watching TV soaps. Students are asked to predict what the soap will be about from the title, or from their previous experience of watching soaps in their native language. This can be responded to orally or in writing, whichever causes the least anxiety. Preactivities can include the following:

> Prequestions: General questions are given before listening, asking the learners to find out a piece of information central to the understanding of the text.

> Do-it-yourself questions: Learners compose and answer their own questions about the listening (this can be also used as a postlistening activity).

> Preface: Students suggest what might have happened before.

For postlesson listening activities, listening to TV soaps offers a rich context for students to practice speaking and writing and a variety of related topics. Activities could resemble the following:

> Oral debate in groups about an issue of disagreement (advanced)

> Class discussion on related topics—culture differences, body language, food, jobs, etc.

> True/false exercises about each program

> Interviews of students who assume the role of any character in the show—in groups or with the whole class

> A class-authored or group-authored soap opera

> Class predictions of the outcome of the next episode or episodes

> Transfer of this approach to other soaps—student-directed

CHAPTER REFLECTION

Using TV soaps is an excellent way of integrating all the previous skills that have been outlined in Chapters 4 (grammar), 5 (writing), 6 (speaking), and 7 (reading). I am a firm believer that English language skills should be integrated, as often as teachers can, in their daily language lessons so that the students can see how all the skill areas depend on each other. This is why I chose listening as the final skill chapter presented in this book. The tasks presented at each stage of the model for strategic listening identify a purpose for listening and a response to that listening. The response can incorporate all the other skill areas, and teachers play an important role in this approach, an approach that is very different from the traditional teacher-fronted approach. The use of TV soaps is an excellent teaching tool for English language teachers in their first years because it can show that TV programs in English can be accessible to students of all levels of proficiency, and that English language learning can even be fun.

CHAPTER NINE

Language Assessment

Teachers of all subjects throughout the world are being asked, if not demanded, to be accountable, and this is especially true in the United States. Teachers have to come up with ways to monitor their students' performance and achievements and make reports to the parents and school authorities that must justify such important decisions as grade promotion, graduation, and whether extra lessons are needed. Teachers usually get the information necessary to make these reports from tests and assessments, which put both teachers and students under lots of pressure. English language teachers have not escaped this pressure, and the pressure is compounded because language assessment is unique: it involves not only written tests but also oral tests. This chapter discusses language assessment from these two perspectives: written and oral testing. The chapter first outlines general theoretical considerations that language teachers need to know when constructing tests and then discusses oral testing. An example of an oral test is included.

Exploratory Break 9.1
Language Assessment

- Have you ever taken a language test (written and/or oral) before?
- If yes, what kind of test was it and where, why, and when did you take it?
- Outline the different aspects of the test—what was difficult, what was easy, what was confusing, and so forth.
- Have you ever compiled a language test (written and/or oral) before? If yes, please describe how you compiled it.

Most teachers would agree that assessing students means assigning grades to the students (a) as evidence that they have taken a course and (b) as an indication of how they did in that course. Another reason teachers assess their students is to determine the various strengths and weaknesses of students. These diagnostic assessments can help teachers plan their courses and tailor the course materials to specific students' needs. This diagnostic assessment can be used as a first step in starting another type of assessment, that of monitoring a student's progress. After an initial diagnosis, teachers want to know how specific students (and their class in general) are doing during the course. This type of assessment can be made at the end of each lesson to monitor whether students are following specific lessons. Teachers can also use this type of monitoring to see if the students are meeting the requirements of the curriculum. This will impact the type of instruction the teacher is providing, for if the students are not making satisfactory progress, the teacher may have to adjust his or her instruction (and maybe provide some extra instruction). This brings us to one more reason why teachers should assess their students: to monitor their own teaching effectiveness. Teaching and assessment are closely linked, for teachers who assess their students well will, in fact, become more effective teachers.

LANGUAGE ASSESSMENT

In language assessment, even more than assessment in other subject areas, teachers have to choose from a vast array of tests. For example, they can choose from traditional-type tests, where students are required to fill in the blanks and the final product is assessed, to more alternative assessment practices, where students are required to perform, produce, or create something and both process and product are assessed. This chapter will address both types, but before this, we must consider holistic aspects of assessment that affect both approaches to testing, namely, issues of reliability and validity and norm-referenced versus criterion-referenced assessment.

Exploratory Break 9.2
Reliability and Validity

Before you start reading about reliability and validity, try to define each:

Reliability . . .

Validity . . .

RELIABILITY AND VALIDITY

A reliable test means that the same test administered in different places will give similar results over time. If, for example, a teacher gives a test to students on a Saturday morning, and then gives the same test the following Saturday, a reliable test should give similar results. Language test validity means that the assessment itself is accurate. In other words, a valid test measures what it claims to measure. For example, if a language teacher claims to be measuring the students' grammatical ability, then the test should not measure other unrelated skill areas such as fluency in spoken language. Additionally, teachers must consider that if a test was testing spoken language proficiency but did not, in fact, require the students to speak, then this would not be considered a valid test. Reliability and validity issues in alternative methods of assessment have also become an important consideration because some traditionalists say their claims of reliability and validity are not strong enough.

Exploratory Break 9.3
Alternative Assessment

- Why do you think it is difficult to construct reliable language tests?
- Why do you think it is difficult to construct valid language tests?

NORM-REFERENCED VERSUS CRITERION-REFERENCED

How do language teachers test their students? Do they have a set of skills that each student will be judged against or do they compare each student's skills in terms of what other students in the same class have attained? The first alternative is called criterion-referenced testing, in which students are assessed in terms of course content, and the second is called norm-referenced testing, in which teachers assess their students in terms of how other students taking the same course have performed on the same test.

Many experienced teachers, although they talk about the distinction between these two types of assessment, more often than not combine both: they look at a grade as an indication of how the student understands the material covered in the course, as well as how the student did in relation to others who have taken the same course and test.

Exploratory Break 9.4
Criterion- and Norm-Referenced Assessment

- How will you assess your students: norm-referenced or criterion-referenced tests, and why?

TYPES OF LANGUAGE ASSESSMENT

When considering how to assess their students, language teachers have an array of different types of tests to choose from and thus must consider what kind of responses they want to elicit from their students. Historically, as Brown and Hudson (1998) have observed, language assessment has moved from discrete-point tests (multiple-choice and true/false tests) in the 50s and 60s to integrative tests (cloze and dictation tests) in the 70s and early 80s, to communicative assessment methods (task-based tests) in the late 80s and 90s. Brown and Hudson provide a useful distinction between the different types of tests available to language teachers: selected- response assessments, constructed-response assessments, and personal-response assessments.

Selected-Response Assessments

In selected-response-type language tests, students do not actually create any language. In written tests, teachers can generally expect responses from their students to include responses from a list of alternative choices given, such as in multiple-choice tests, true/false tests, and matching tests. These are the most common types of test items.

Exploratory Break 9.5
Selected-Response Assessment

- Which type of selected-response assessment is easy to construct for a teacher and why?
- Which type of selected-response assessment is difficult to construct and why?
- Which type of selected-response assessment is easiest to score and why?

Multiple-choice tests offer the test takers a choice of one correct answer out of a number of "distracters" that are incorrect.

Exploratory Break 9.6
Multiple-Choice Tests

- List some advantages and some disadvantages of multiple-choice tests and compare your answers to what you read next.
- Two advantages of using multiple-choice tests are that they are easy to score either by hand or by machine, and the scoring is reliable. However, one major disadvantage is that these tests could promote guessing, and this can have an effect on the score. Multiple-choice tests only check recognition knowledge, and you cannot be sure students actually understand the question because they do not have to generate an answer.

True/false tests offer the test takers a choice between two items, one true and one false, from a sample of language.

Exploratory Break 9.7
True/False Tests

- List some advantages and some disadvantages of true/false tests and compare your answers to what you read next.
- The advantage of using true/false tests is that students are quickly assessed on how they choose between two alternatives and whether they understand the question. These types of tests must be carefully designed to minimize guessing, a major disadvantage of choosing between only two alternatives, to ensure that you are testing exactly what language item you want.

Matching tests present the test takers with two lists of language items (vocabulary words, idioms, or phrases), and they must match each item from one list to an item on the other list.

Exploratory Break 9.8
Matching Tests

- List some advantages and some disadvantages of matching tests and compare your answers to what you read next.

- Even though some may say that matching tests can also encourage guessing, they have a much lower instance of this, as one guess can lead to a chain of incorrect answers. Thus, students are tested about their knowledge of matching one set of facts with another. Vocabulary, more than other skills, lends itself to this type of test.

Constructed-Response Assessments

Constructed-response assessments require that test takers actually produce something, usually in writing and/or speech. The main production types of tests in this category are short-answer tests, essay tests, fill-in tests, and oral tests.

Short-answer item tests require students to supply a word or a sentence in response to a question or a statement that they must complete.

Exploratory Break 9.9
Short-Answer Tests

- List some advantages and some disadvantages of short-answer item tests and compare your answers to what you read next.
- One advantage that short-answer item tests have over multiple-choice tests is that students must generate an answer, as opposed to recognizing an answer as in multiple-choice testing. However, a disadvantage of this type of testing is that the tests are difficult to score: the longer the response required, the more difficult it is to score, and students may produce different answers. Thus the reliability of the short-answer test can be questioned.

Essay item tests are used when teachers want students to generate long answers in the form of a paragraph or a complete essay (usually consisting of five paragraphs).

Exploratory Break 9.10
Essay Tests

- List some advantages and some disadvantages of essay item tests and compare your answers to what you read next.

- One advantage of an essay item test is that it requires students to organize and synthesize their thoughts on a particular subject (depending on the essay question). As they compose their essay, students must also evaluate what information to include and not to include. However, herein is a disadvantage: writing an essay in itself is difficult. Essays are also difficult for teachers to score because of the subjective nature of what a good essay is.

Fill-in tests require the test taker to provide a missing word (the language item is removed and replaced with a blank; e.g., verb past tense removed). These can be as complex as a cloze test where each *n*th word or phrase is removed or as simple as a single-word fill-in.

Exploratory Break 9.11
Fill-in Tests

- List some advantages and some disadvantages of fill-in tests and compare your answers to what you read next.
- Fill-in tests are easy to construct but have the disadvantage of what to do if the test takers provide different answers, especially with cloze tests. So teachers may want to consider limiting the range of possible answers by providing the first letter of the missing word or phrase.

Oral tests require a tester to set a task for the test taker to perform. This task demands English speech, and the tester notes the performance of the test taker and assigns a score. It sounds straightforward, but it is not because it is more difficult to assess spoken English with exact accuracy than to assess other language skills, such as reading or writing English.

Exploratory Break 9.12
Oral Tests

- Why would it be more difficult to test oral English rather than reading or writing English?
- Have you ever taken an oral test in a foreign language? If so, describe your experience.
- Have you ever constructed an oral test? If so, describe how you constructed the test.

Oral testing is much more difficult than written testing because speaking is a very complex skill requiring the simultaneous use of a number of different abilities that often develop at different rates: pronunciation, grammar, vocabulary, fluency, the ease and speed of the flow of speech, and comprehension in oral communication. So, oral tests must provide a reasonably consistent assessment of the test taker's performance to indicate his or her proficiency.

Personal-Response Assessments

Similar to constructed-response-type assessment, personal-response assessment requires test takers to produce language but in a personally constructed manner, such as portfolios or self- or peer assessment.

Portfolios require students to gather in one place different representations or collections of representative work they have completed over a period of time. Contents can include essays and drafts of essays, other test examples that showcase their achievements, diary writings, and self-appraisal example essays. For example, in essay writing with portfolio assessment, students keep the writing they have done over the course of a term or more, including early drafts. Then they analyze their writing to understand the progress they have made. Next, they select from among their pieces of writing to compile a collection that demonstrates the path of their writing journey. Last, they prepare an introduction to the portfolio in which they present their findings.

Exploratory Break 9.13
Portfolios

- List some advantages and some disadvantages of portfolio tests and compare your answers to what you read next.
- Self- or peer assessment requires either students themselves to rate their own language abilities or their peers to rate their language ability. For example, peer feedback is now common in writing classes. To rate their own language ability, students would go through the test, such as a reading test, and decide how they would rate their reading and comprehension of that passage. For listening comprehension assessment, they would listen to a tape recording (audio or video) and decide how well they understood it. For speaking, they could record their voices (again audio or video) and decide how well they speak the language. For writing, they would write and then decide how good their composition is. These could all be assessed by peers, too.

Exploratory Break 9.14
Self- or Peer Assessment

- List some advantages and some disadvantages of self- or peer assessment and compare your answers to what you read next.
- Self-assessment is easy to administer and it is quick. Also, students take more ownership in the assessment process because they are more involved in the process, and they may become more motivated to improve their language proficiency as a result. On the negative side, both teachers and students may wonder if the students themselves are capable of assessing their own proficiency levels: they may overestimate or underestimate their levels. Also, some peer assessment may be perceived as a waste of time and unfair by the students if the teacher is not involved in this assessment process. However, I have found that critiquing the writing of fellow students helps learners better understand and internalize criteria for successful writing.

Exploratory Break 9.15
Constructing Language Tests

When you are writing a test for your students, what general guidelines do you follow (if any) when constructing the test? (Compare these to the following guidelines.)

The following three guidelines (adapted from Aebersold & Field, 1997) are useful to remember when writing a test, regardless of the type of test or the reason for the test.

GUIDELINES FOR WRITING ENGLISH LANGUAGE TESTS

Keep the course objectives clearly in mind. Teachers usually assess their students so their students can demonstrate what they have learned as a result of taking a course. So, when teachers are writing a test for this purpose, they should always keep track of the course objectives they set and explained to their students, and they should not test material that has not been covered in some way during the course.

Carefully match the test to what is to be tested. Connected to the first guideline (in the previous paragraph) is that the test itself should be similar to the curriculum of the course the students just completed. This concerns the validity (see previous discussion) of a test. For example, if a teacher just completed a unit of math that was devoted to problem solving, then one would expect a test that covered problem-solving questions only. Thus, content and construct validity would not be a concern.

Recognize the potential for bias and variation. Teachers must realize that their students come from different cultural backgrounds and that some types of tests may be biased in favor of certain cultural groups, while the same tests may disadvantage other groups. Also, certain tests (the entire test or parts of the test) may be offensive to a certain subgroup of students who are taking the examination. When teachers present negative stereotypes of certain groups in tests, they offend and, worse, distress the examinees from that subgroup, which can lead to a poor performance on the test. One way teachers can reduce this possible bias or variation is to provide different types of assessment, both traditional and nontraditional, to determine the success of a student.

A Strategic Approach to Assessment of Spoken English

English language teachers sometimes need some kind of oral test to determine either where they can place ESL students into an ESL program or when to consider moving their kids out of ESL placements. The question is, how can they do this reliably? The argument is basically between linguistic competence assessment and pragmatic assessment. In linguistic competence assessment, a specific list of words and phrases is prepared for the examiner to listen for in the response to ensure dependable scoring. The raters all follow the same general procedures by devoting approximately the same time to the average interview: speaking to the candidate at about the same rate of speech, maintaining the same level of difficulty in the questions they ask, and applying the same general rating standards. My motivation for making a new oral test was that it would be fairly reliable and valid in placing students into and out of programs. I have found that ready-made commercial tests did not suit my needs. I have used this oral test many times in my 27 years of English language teaching.

Example of Oral Test

This oral test has three main sections, as follows: Section A is an introduction and assesses a speaker's grammar. Section B assesses a student's ability to give opinions in English. Section C assesses a student's ability to use English creatively, analytically, and critically. Each section is outlined below.

Section A: Introduction (structure and grammar)

1. Please introduce yourself by stating your name, age, education, family background, and present occupation.

2. What do you like to do in your free time?

3. What did you do last weekend?

4. What will you do after this interview?

5. Report at least two things different people said to you last week.

Section B: Pictorial/Opinion

Student is given a picture or photograph.

1. Please describe the picture (what do you see?).

2. Make up a possible story for the picture.

3. What is your opinion about (topic related to the picture)?

Section C: Creative, Analytical, and Critical Use of Language

The following two questions are examples—teachers can add to these, making questions increasingly difficult depending on the objective of the oral test.

1. If you went to live in another country, which of your customs would you like to keep and why?

2. What changes do you expect to occur in this (your) country in the next ten years?

Scoring Procedures

I use the following scoring procedures to grade the above oral test:

Students will be scored 0 to 4 points in each section, but please take note of the following:

Pronunciation is not a factor unless it inhibits communication.

Listening comprehension should be considered in each section, with one point being deducted if the speaker continually asks for repetition of the question.

Section A: Accuracy

Correct grammar and correct information in the test taker's answer are the main foci of this section. Accuracy means the correctness of the grammar in comparison to that of a speaker of standard American English. Rather than consider the whole spectrum of grammar, attend to the structure, verb tenses, and subject-verb agreement in rough order of importance.

4 points: Grammar is correctly used along with appropriate answers given. Further, the test taker volunteers more information than was required and speaks without undue hesitation and with confidence.

3 points: Grammar is appropriately used 90 percent of the time. The test taker might correct errors. There could be some hesitation or a request for a question to be repeated.

2 points: Grammar is 60–90 percent accurate. There is more hesitation.

1 point: There is a grammar error in almost every sentence.

0 points: Every sentence has a grammar error, and the responses are short. Or the test taker has no idea how to answer.

Section B: Pictorial/Opinion

The emphasis in this section is on communication.

4 points: The test taker responds freely and without undue hesitation, continues when requested, and is highly productive; language flows until ideas are exhausted.

3 points: The test taker responds with one or more spontaneous remarks and continues with more when challenged by the interviewer. Test taker makes some grammatical errors but they are more like slips of the tongue.

2 points: Similar response to those receiving 4 and 3 points; however, makes many grammar mistakes, enough so that it could be distracting from comprehending the content of the answer.

1 point: The test taker does not respond until encouraged, and does not really continue after that. The tester must work too hard with the test taker.

0 points: The interviewer is just going through the motions.

Section C: Creative, Analytical, and Critical Use of Language

The emphasis in this section is on fluency.

4 points: The test taker responds freely and without undue hesitation, continues when requested, and is highly productive; language flows until ideas are exhausted.

3 points: The test taker responds with one or more spontaneous remarks and continues with more when challenged by the interviewer. Test taker makes some grammatical errors but they are more like slips of the tongue.

2 points: Similar response to those receiving 4 and 3 points; however, makes many grammar mistakes, enough so that it could be distracting from comprehending the content of the answer.

1 point: The test taker does not respond until encouraged, and does not really continue after that. The tester must work too hard with the test taker.

0 points: The interviewer is just going through the motions.

(Note: For ease of scoring, if the test taker gets 1 or 0 points in Section A and 1 or 0 points in Section B, then stop; otherwise, continue.)

Score Sheet Oral Communication Test

Section	*Score*				
A	0	1	2	3	4
B	0	1	2	3	4
C	0	1	2	3	4
Total	___				

Exploratory Break 9.16
Create Your Own Language Test

The oral test previously outlined supports the notion that English language teachers can construct their own tests that meet their own needs and best suit their own context.

- Design your own oral interview either using components of the example by modifying each component or making a completely new one.
- Explain how and why you designed your own oral test.

CHAPTER REFLECTION

This chapter has outlined various methods of assessment at the disposal of language teachers. The chapter discussed tests such as multiple-choice, true/false, and fill-in-the-blank-type traditional tests, and alternative assessment instruments such as interviews, portfolios, and self- and peer assessment tests, the latter being a bit more time-consuming and costly to use. Language teachers should also remember that the goal of language assessment is not just assessing a student's language proficiency, but it is also to teach. In the case of more alternative assessment instruments, students of second and foreign languages may be encouraged and motivated to take a more active part in their language education and assessment as a result of having to compile a portfolio of their various achievements and by having to assess their own language ability or a peer's ability. As a result, second and foreign language students may even be better prepared to take standardized tests because they are more aware of learning as a process of discovery and that a standardized test is only one measure of that learning.

CHAPTER TEN

Professional Development

Many teachers in their first year assume that once they have graduated from the teacher education program they just finished, they will have learned all there is to know about teaching the English language and they will never have to go back. All experienced teachers realize that this could not be further from the truth and that they will never know all there is to know about teaching language. The one thing they do know is that changes will take place in technology, curriculum, and teaching methods, and new theories will emerge. What you learned in your teacher education course one year or even five years ago may not be relevant now because of the pace of developments (Richards & Farrell, 2005). For example, language teachers always need to update their knowledge of recent research in all language areas, such as second language acquisition research, composition research, technology developments, and assessment developments (Richards & Farrell, 2005). How are language teachers supposed to keep up with all these changes and remain competent teachers throughout their careers so that they can provide the best possible education for their students? This chapter will give you some tools that you can use to reflect on your accumulating experiences and that you can use for future action as a professional language teacher. In this chapter, I discuss the concept of reflective practice as professional development, and I outline various activities that you can use for your future professional development as an English language teacher. First, it is time for you to take a look at *your* professional development needs in Exploratory Break 10.1.

Exploratory Break 10.1
Professional Development Needs Assessment

Try to answer the following professional development questions.

- What does teacher development mean to you?
- What do you think is the best way to keep informed about developments in English language teaching?
- Where can you get ideas about teaching methods and techniques?
- Where can you get information about language?
- Where can you learn more about teaching?
- How can you improve your teaching skills?
- Which areas do you think you need to develop in your teaching?

Compare your answers with those suggested in the next section.

PROFESSIONAL DEVELOPMENT NEEDS

In this section, I outline some possible answers to the professional development needs assessment in Exploratory Break 10.1. I hope you find these suggestions useful; they are based on my 27 years as a language teacher educator. During that time, I surveyed many English language teachers in many diverse settings and asked them the same questions I just posed to you. Do you agree with their answers?

What does teacher development mean to you?

Some possible answers could be the following:

Improve language skills

Improve teaching skills

Become a better teacher

Keep up-to-date with what is happening in English language teaching

Develop more methods and techniques about teaching

Become more aware about theory behind practice

What do you think is the best way to keep informed about developments in English language teaching?

Some possible answers could be the following:

Read English language teaching magazines

Read academic journals in the field

Talk to colleagues

Attend conferences

Attend workshops

Take short courses or inservice courses

Read books in the field

Where can you get ideas about teaching methods and techniques?

Some possible answers could be the following:

Attend talks or demonstrations by other teachers (brown bag lunches)

Attend workshops

Attend short courses

Attend inservice courses at your institution

Read textbooks and teachers' manuals

Attend conferences

Read teacher resource books on teaching theory

Read academic journals

Read teaching magazines

Where can you get information about language?

Some possible answers could be the following:

Read grammar books

Ask colleagues

Read teachers' books

Read textbooks

Look up words in dictionaries

Where can you learn more about teaching?

Some possible answers could be the following:

From observing your own experiences in the next years

From other teachers

Get more training

How can you improve your teaching skills?

Some possible answers could be the following:

By observing other teachers (peers)

By being observed by other teachers (peers)

By writing a journal about teaching

By taping (video and/or audio) your classes

By observation by more experienced colleagues

Group discussions with other teachers (informal)

Group discussions with other teachers (formal)

Get student feedback

Attend seminars, workshops, and conferences

Which areas do you think you need to develop in your teaching?

Some possible answers could be the following:

Obtain new ideas for classroom activities

Get more experience teaching different courses

Develop your communication skills

Improve your English language abilities

Become more aware of what is happening in your classroom

Learn more about the theory behind language teaching and learning

This last question becomes the focus of the remainder of this chapter: as teachers in their first years gain experience, they must also reflect on this experience if they want to develop fully as teachers and future teacher mentors. One way of doing this is to engage in reflective practice throughout their careers.

PROFESSIONAL DEVELOPMENT AND REFLECTIVE PRACTICE PROFESSIONAL DEVELOPMENT

Richards and Farrell (2005) have suggested the following areas that language teachers should consider when looking at their professional development:

Subject-Matter Knowledge. Language teachers need to keep up knowledge related to the discipline of language teaching. For example, they need to keep updated on trends in English grammar, discourse analysis, phonology, testing, second language acquisition research, methodology, curriculum development, and the other areas that define the professional knowledge base of language teaching.

Pedagogical Expertise. Teachers always need to master new areas of teaching and add to their teaching specializations so that they can teach different skill areas to learners of different ages and backgrounds.

Self-Awareness. Language teachers must have knowledge of themselves as teachers. They must understand their principles and values, and be able to access their areas of strength and weakness.

Understanding of Learners. Language teachers must be able to deepen their understanding of their learners and their learning styles, problems, and difficulties, and consider different ways of making content more accessible to learners.

Understanding of Curriculum and Materials. Language teachers must also deepen their understanding of the curriculum they use and constantly develop their instructional materials.

Career Advancement. Language teachers must never give up the quest to acquire knowledge and expertise necessary for personal advancement and promotion, so that some day they can mentor other language teachers in their first years.

REFLECTIVE PRACTICE

In recent times, teachers have been encouraged to reflect on every aspect of their teaching (Farrell, 2004a), because teachers are often unaware of what they do when they teach and how their teaching influences their students' levels of learning. Reflective practice for language teachers is a systematic and structured process in which teachers look into something concrete within their teaching and their students' learning, with the overall goal of changing for the purpose of becoming a more effective teacher. For the purposes of this chapter, I consider reflection to be in practice when a teacher seeks answers to the following questions (Farrell, 2004a):

What is he or she doing in the classroom (method)?

Why is he or she doing this (reason)?

What was the result?

Will he or she change anything based on the information gathered from answering the first two questions (justification)?

Reflection in teaching generally refers to teachers learning to subject their own beliefs of teaching and learning to a critical analysis, and thus take more responsibility for their actions in the classroom (Farrell, 2004a).

A STRATEGIC APPROACH TO PROFESSIONAL DEVELOPMENT

Just as I have outlined a strategic approach to teaching the skill areas of English language, I also now offer you a strategic approach to your professional development for the remainder of your teaching career. I challenge you now to take charge of your own teaching and development by becoming your own researcher. In other words, I hope you become a teacher-researcher for the remainder of your career. I offer you the following methods of gathering research so that you can become a reflective practitioner:

Action research

Critical incident analysis

Journals (diary writing)

Observation tasks (self, peer)

Teacher development groups

Exploratory Break 10.2
Opportunities for Reflection and Development

When providing opportunities for teachers to reflect, the model of reflective practice in this chapter has suggested the following activities that individual teachers, pairs of teachers, or a team of teachers can use:

Action research

Critical incident analysis

Teaching journals

Observation tasks (self, peer)

Teacher development groups

- What do you think a teacher (or pair or group of teachers) would have to do in each activity?
- Which activity would be easiest and which would be hardest for teachers to use in order to reflect on their work?
- Try to think of other reflection activities that teachers could use when reflecting on their work.

ACTION RESEARCH

Action research is, as McFee (1993) says, "research into (1) a particular kind of practice—one in which there is a craft-knowledge, and (2) is research based on a particular model of knowledge and research with action as an outcome . . . this knowledge is practical knowledge" (p. 178). I have found the following cycle of action research useful (Richards & Farrell, 2005):

1. Plan (problem identification): A teacher identifies a problem.

2. Research (literature review): The teacher reads about what has been done before about the problem.

3. Observe (collecting data): The teacher collects data about the problem—classroom, surveys, and so on.

4. Reflect (analysis): The teacher analyzes the collected data to make informed decisions about teaching.

5. Act (redefining the problem): The teacher makes changes as a result of Steps 1–4 and then starts the cycle all over again to see the impact of these decisions.

The language teacher sees a need to investigate a problem (perceived or otherwise) and then starts to plan how to investigate ways of solving this problem. The teacher starts reading some background literature on the problem to give him or her ideas on how to solve the problem. Of course, this "research" cycle can include talking to other colleagues about the concern, as they may have some advice to offer. The teacher then plans a strategy to collect data now that the problem has been identified and researched. Once the data has been collected, the teacher then analyzes and reflects on it and makes a data-driven decision to take some action. The final step in this spiraling cycle of research and action is problem redefinition. In this way, language teachers can take more responsibility for the decisions they make in their classes. However, these decisions are now informed decisions, not just based on feelings or impulse.

Exploratory Break 10.3
Action Research

- Try to think of any question or action research project you think you would like to attempt. Make a list—an example could be an investigation of the type of questions you ask, the amount of time you wait (wait time) after you ask a student a question, or what kinds of groups work best in your classroom (gender, age, number, etc.).
- Now that you have identified a problem or a focus for your action research project, examine the action research reflective cycle summarized next and see if you can complete one cycle of this action research:

Identify a problem (or focus)

Collect data systematically (information) about the problem

Examine, analyze, and interpret the information gathered in order to reflect on what the information tells you

Act on the information by making some changes in your teaching to improve practice

Reflect on the changes by going through one more cycle

CRITICAL INCIDENT ANALYSIS

Some educators have suggested that by reflecting on critical incidents in a formal manner, it may be possible for teachers to uncover new understandings of the teaching and learning process. A critical incident is any unplanned event that happens in a class (Richards & Farrell, 2005). Analyzing critical incidents can give you a deeper understanding of your teaching as you begin to examine the underlying basis for your decisions during class. Incidents that are critical to some beginning teachers may be commonplace to more experienced teachers, so Exploratory Break 10.4 will yield different answers to different teachers.

Exploratory Break 10.4
Critical Incidents

Review any critical incidents you have documented in your teaching journal or you can think of now, and try to answer the following questions about these critical incidents:

- What was the incident that happened in your class?
- Why was this incident important to you?
- What happened exactly in the lesson that made this event important?
- How did you react (did you react?) at the time of the incident?
- Did you stop teaching?
- What does this critical incident tell you about your beliefs and values as they relate to teaching?

TEACHING JOURNALS

Teaching journals are an excellent tool for reflection (Farrell, 2004a), are simple to create and maintain, and can promote the development of reflective teaching. Individual teachers, pairs of teachers, or teams or groups of teachers can use teaching journals when reflecting on their work. Teachers can write journals at any time of the working day (although I usually like to write a journal after a class or a significant event in case I forget what happened later) and even after work to reflect on their teaching. In their journals, teachers can record criticisms, doubts, frustrations, questions, the joys of teaching, the results of experiments, and just about anything else, as it is difficult to separate our working lives from our teaching lives. I find that writing in a teaching journal regularly can also be cathartic, especially if the journal is used to let off steam about some frustrations encountered during the teaching day and during your first years on the job. As I pointed out in Chapter 1, learning to teach is an anxiety-provoking experience and a complex undertaking. So documenting some of your experiences in order to look later at your writing to examine for patterns of thought may be a worthwhile reflective experience. Rather than always wondering what is happening during these first years, you can examine your writing and see exactly what occurred and what you want to do about it.

You can also write about your successful teaching in the classroom as well as the problems that occurred. By writing about what went wrong and what went well in our classrooms, we can look for patterns in both to see if we can come up with reasons why we perceived these classroom events as having been successful or not. In this way, we can define for ourselves what "good" and "bad" teaching is, rather than wait for a supervisor who is not familiar with the class or teaching to do so. In this way also, our reflections on our practice are more systematic, and we can thus make more informed decisions about our teaching. We can use our teaching journal to explore and examine our beliefs about teaching and learning and our actual classroom practices and see if there is a gap between these two. So, by writing regularly about our work, we can begin to see patterns about how we think and believe and about how we teach (Richards & Farrell, 2005). A more detailed analysis of teaching journals can even reveal if there are any inconsistencies between our teaching beliefs and our actual classroom practices.

Exploratory Break 10.5
Teaching Journal

Now would be a good time to begin your teaching journal. In order to start, you must consider the following questions first:

- Will you use a computer or an ordinary notebook?
- Will you organize your writing or will you just freewrite your thoughts and rearrange these later?
- Who is your audience: yourself, a peer, and/or an instructor?
- What will you focus your writing on: a lesson, a technique or method, a theory, a question posed, or some aspect of your job outside the classroom?
- How regularly will you write: after a lesson, daily, or once a week?
- How regularly will you review what you have written: every two or three weeks?

CLASSROOM OBSERVATIONS

Classroom observations occur when teachers look at what goes on in their classrooms by reviewing concrete data related to their classes

(Farrell, 2004a). Individual teachers, pairs, or groups of teachers can observe classes. Pairs of teachers can also team up to discuss teaching in the form of critical friendships. These critical friends can challenge each other in positive ways in a safe environment in such a way that both friends grow as teachers. The main emphasis here is on the friend rather than on the criticism. Groups of teachers can also observe each other's classes. Classroom observation should be nonjudgmental because making judgments on one another only blocks development.

Exploratory Break 10.6
Classroom Observations

- Have you ever experienced a classroom observation?
- If your answer is yes, was it positive or negative?
- If it was positive, why was it so? If it was negative, why was it so?
- Describe your experience.
- Ask a friend/colleague/peer to join you in a critical friendship.
- Ask your critical friend to observe you teach without giving any feedback (this will get you used to having another peer in your room).
- You can also observe your friend teaching.
- Draw up a list of observation "rules" that both observers should follow when you conduct further classroom observations.

TEACHER DEVELOPMENT GROUPS

Group discussions, in which teachers talk to other teachers, are another means for teachers interested in practicing reflection (Farrell, 2004a). In this case, teachers come together with the aim of sharing some of their thoughts on teaching and their work. The advantage of seeking out other teachers, especially for teachers in their first years, is that teachers often discover they have similar experiences, joys, problems, and challenges. By forming a group, they can get moral support, empathy, and even sympathy in some cases, from other like-minded professionals. They can also see other ways of approaching different issues, such as problem students, introducing new curriculum initiatives, or dealing with the administration. I think teachers in their first years should make it a priority to seek out other teachers—both experienced and beginning teachers—so that they can avoid the isolation that many teachers tend to endure (some may say suffer) during much of their career.

Exploratory Break 10.7
Teacher Group Discussion

- Have you ever participated in discussions with other teachers on a regular basis? If so, please describe your experiences: What did you talk about? What was the interaction like? What did you gain from the discussions? What do you think could have been done better in the group?

When setting up a teacher development group, participants should consider the following questions as a guide:

- What is the purpose of the group?
- How many members will the group consist of (pairs are possible, too)?
- What roles will each member have (including who will be the leader or facilitator)?
- Where will the group meet and how long will the meetings be?
- How will the group arrange for confidentiality concerning issues that arise in the group meetings?
- Will the group members engage in classroom observations ?
- Will each member of the group write a teaching journal?
- Will the group engage in action research projects?
- How will the group generate topics for reflection?

CHAPTER REFLECTION

This chapter is a beginning rather than an end to your exploration of English language teaching in your first years. I have offered various ways in which you can continue your reflections and explorations of your teaching so that you will continue to make informed decisions in your classroom and your students can become more reflective learners. I hope you will continue in the teaching profession for many more years to come and always remain curious about what it means to be a teacher of the English language to native speakers and nonnative speakers of English. One of your greatest challenges over the next years of teaching the English language will be to keep up with the many developments in the field. One way of doing this is to read journals in the field and attend workshops, seminars, conferences, and inservice training programs. Another way, as suggested in this chapter, is to keep talking to other English language teachers both inside your school and in the school district so you can compare your teaching methods to what other teachers are doing. Remember, teaching is a lonely profession because teachers usually do not talk about what they do to other teachers—maybe because of a fear of being exposed in some way. If you retain the feeling of excitement and exploration from your teacher education days, you will have a long and fruitful teaching career.

References

Aebersold, J. A., & Field, M. L. (1997). *From reader to reading teacher.* Cambridge, UK: Cambridge University Press.

Anthony, H. M., Pearson, P. D., & Raphael, T. E. (1993). Reading comprehension: A selected review. In L. M. Cleary & M. D. Linn (Eds.), *Linguistics for teachers.* New York: McGraw-Hill.

Bailey, K. M. (1996). The best-laid plans: Teachers' in-class decisions to depart from their lesson plans. In K. M. Bailey & D. Nunan (Eds.), *Voices from the language classroom: Qualitative research in second language classrooms* (pp. 15–40). New York: Cambridge University Press.

Barnes, D. (1976). *From communication to curriculum.* Middlesex, UK: Penguin.

Brown, H. D. (1994). *Teaching by principles.* Englewood Cliffs, NJ: Prentice Hall Regents.

Brown, J. D., & Hudson, T. (1998). Alternatives in language assessment. *TESOL Quarterly, 32*(4), 653–675.

Bullough, R. V., & Baughman, K. (1993). Continuity and change in teacher development: A first year teacher after five years. *Journal of Teacher Education, 44,* 86–95.

Calderhead, J. (1992). Induction: A research perspective on the professional growth of the newly qualified teacher. In *The induction of newly appointed teachers, general teaching for England and Wales* (pp. 5–21).

Carew, J., & Lightfoot, S. L. (1979). *Beyond bias: Perspectives on classrooms.* Cambridge, MA: Harvard University Press.

Carrell, P. L. (1998). Can reading strategies be successfully taught? *ARAL, 21*(1), 1–20.

Carroll, L. (1963). *Alice's adventures in wonderland.* New York: Macmillan.

Celce-Murcia, M. (1991). *Teaching English as a second or foreign language.* Boston: Heinle & Heinle.

Conner, U., & Kaplan, R. (1987). *Writing across languages: Analysis of L2 test.* Reading, MA: Addison-Wesley.

Cross, D. (1991). *A practical handbook of language teaching.* London, UK: Dotesios.

Dunkel, P. (1991). Listening in the native and second/foreign language: Toward an integration of research and practice. *TESOL Quarterly, 25*(3), 431–457.

Farrell, T. S. C. (2000). Activating prior knowledge in L2 reading: The teacher's role. *Guidelines, 22*(1), 10–16.

Farrell, T. S. C. (2002). Lesson planning. In J. C. Richards & W. A. Renandya (Eds.), *Methodology in language teaching: An anthology of current practice* (pp. 30–39). New York: Cambridge University Press.

Farrell, T. S. C. (2004a). *Reflective practice in action.* Thousand Oaks, CA: Corwin.

Farrell, T. S. C. (2004b). *Reflecting on classroom communication in Asia.* Singapore: Longman.

Ferris, D. (1995). Teaching students to self-edit. *TESOL Quarterly, 21*(2), 279–304.

Field, J. (2000). Finding one's way in the fog: Listening strategies and second language learners. *Modern English Teacher, 9*(1), 29–34.

Field, J. (2002). The changing face of listening. In J. C. Richards & W. A. Renandya (Eds.), *Methodology in language teaching: An anthology of current practice* (pp. 242–247). New York: Cambridge University Press.

Fuller, F. F., & Brown, O. H. (1975). Becoming a teacher. In K. Ryan (Ed.), *Teacher education: The seventy-fourth yearbook of the National Society for the Study of Education* (pp. 25–51). Chicago: National Society for the Study of Education.

Grabe, W. (2002). Dilemmas for the development of second language reading abilities. In J. C. Richards & W. A. Renandya (Eds.), *Methodology in language teaching: An anthology of current practice* (pp. 276–286). New York: Cambridge University Press.

Hargreaves, A. (1994). *Changing teachers, changing times: Teachers' work and culture in a postmodern age.* Trowbridge, UK: Cassell.

Harley, B. (1989). Functional grammar in French immersion: A classroom experiment. *Applied Linguistics, 10,* 331–348.

Helgesen, M., Brown, S., & Mandeville, T. (1987). *English firsthand.* Tokyo: Lingual House.

Herbert, J. (2002). PracTESOL: It's not what you say, but how you say it! In J. C. Richards & W. A. Renandya (Eds.), *Methodology in language teaching: An anthology of current practice* (pp. 188–200). New York: Cambridge University Press.

Hunter, M., & Russell, D. (1977). How can I plan more effective lessons? *Instructor, 87,* 74–75.

Jacobs, G. M., & Farrell, T. S. C. (2002). Understanding and implementing the CLT (communicative language teaching) paradigm. *RELC Journal, 34*(1), 5–30.

Jacobs, G. M., & Hall, S. (2002). Implementing cooperative learning. In J. C. Richards & W. A. Renandya (Eds.), *Methodology in language teaching: An anthology of current practice* (pp. 52–58). New York: Cambridge University Press.

Johnson, K. E. (1996). The vision versus the reality: The tensions of the TESOL practicum. In D. Freeman & J. Richards (Eds.), *Teacher learning in language teaching* (pp. 30–49). New York: Cambridge University Press.

Jordan, R. (1990). Pyramid discussion. *ELTJ, 44*(1), 48.

Jordell, K. O. (1987). Structural and personal influences in the socialization of beginning teachers. *Teaching and Teacher Education, 3,* 165–176.

Kagan, S. (1992). *Cooperative learning.* San Clemente, CA: Kagan Cooperative Learning.

Larsen-Freeman, D. (1991). Teaching grammar. In Celce-Murcia, M. (Ed.), *Teaching English as a second or foreign language* (pp. 279–296). Boston: Heinle & Heinle.

Leki, I. (1991a). Teaching second language writing: Where we seem to be. *English Teaching Forum, 29,* 8–11.

Leki, I. (1991b). The preferences of ESL students for error correction in college level writing classes. *Foreign Language Annals, 24,* 203–217.

Leki, I. (1991c). Twenty-five years of contrastive rhetoric: Text analysis and writing pedagogies. *TESOL Quarterly, 25,* 123–143.

Lewis, M. (2002). Classroom management. In J. C. Richards & W. Renandya (Eds.), *Methodology in language teaching: An anthology of current practice* (pp. 40–48). New York: Cambridge University Press.

Liang, X., Mohan, B. A., & Early, M. (1998). Issues of cooperative learning in ESL classes: A literature review. *TESL Canada Journal, 15*(2), 13–23.

Lortie, D. C. (1975). *Schoolteacher: A sociological study.* Chicago: University of Chicago Press.

Lund, R. J. (1990). A taxonomy for teaching second language listening. *Foreign Language Annals, 23,* 105–115.

Malderez, A., & Bodoczky, C. (1999). *Mentor courses: A resource book for teacher-trainers.* Cambridge, UK: Cambridge University Press.

Maynard, T., & Furlong, J. (1995). Learning to teach and models of mentoring. In T. Kelly & A. Mayes (Eds.), *Issues in mentoring* (pp. 10–24). London: Routledge.

McFee, G. (1993). Reflections on the nature of action-research. *Cambridge Journal of Education, 23*(2), 173–183.

Mendelsohn, D. (1995). Applying learning strategies in the second/foreign language listening comprehension lesson. In D. Mendelsohn & J. Rubin (Eds.), *A guide for the teaching of second language listening* (pp. 132–149). San Diego, CA: Dominie Press.

Mendonca, C. O., & Johnson, K. E. (1994). Peer review negotiations: Revision activities in ESL writing instruction. *TESOL Quarterly, 28*(4), 745–769.

Myers, S. (1997). Teaching writing as a process and teaching sentence-level syntax: Reformulation as ESL composition feedback. *TESL-EJ, 2*(4), 1–16.

Myles, J. (2002). Second language writing and research: The writing process and error analysis in student texts. *TESL-EJ, 6*(2), 1–20.

Nunan, D. (2002). Listening in language learning. In J. C. Richards & W. Renandya (Eds.), *Methodology in language teaching: An anthology of current practice* (pp. 238–241). New York: Cambridge University Press.

Odell, S. J., & Ferraro, D. P. (1992). Teacher mentoring and teacher retention. *Journal of Teacher Education, 43,* 200–204.

Oxford, R. L. (1990). *Language learning strategies: What every teacher should know.* New York: Newbury House.

Philips, S. (1983). *The invisible culture: Communication in classroom and community on the Warm Springs Indian Reservation.* Prospect Heights, IL: Waveland Press.

Pica, T., Young, R., & Doughty, C. (1987). The impact of interaction on comprehension. *TESOL Quarterly, 21*(4), 737–758.

Raimes, A. (2002). Ten steps in planning a writing course and training teachers of writing. In J. C. Richards & W. Renandya (Eds.), *Methodology in language teaching: An anthology of current practice* (pp. 306–314). New York: Cambridge University Press.

Richards, J. C. (1998). *Beyond methods.* Cambridge, UK: Cambridge University Press.

Richards, J. C., & Farrell, T. S. C. (2005). *Professional development for language teachers.* New York: Cambridge University Press.

Richards, J. C. (1990). *The language teaching matrix.* New York: Cambridge University Press.

Richards, J. C., & Renandya, W. (Eds.). (2002). *Methodology in language teaching: An anthology of current practice.* New York: Cambridge University Press.

Rodby, J. (1990). The ESL writer and the kaleidoscopic self. *Writing Instructor, 10,* 42–50.

Rost, M. (1990). *Listening in language learning.* London: Longman.

Rost, M. (1991). *Listening in action.* Hemel Hempstead, Herts, UK: Prentice-Hall.

Sacks, H., Schegloff, E., & Jefferson, G. (1974). A simplest systematics for the organization of turn-taking in conversation. *Language, 50*(4), 696–735.

Schegloff, E. A. (1981). Discourse as an interactional achievement: Some uses of "uh huh" and other things that come between sentences. In D. Tannen (Ed.), *Analyzing discourse: Text and talk* (pp. 71–93). Washington, DC: Georgetown University Press.

Schegloff, E. A., Jefferson, G., & Sacks, H. (1977). The preference for self-correction in the organization of repair in conversation. *Language, 53*(2), 361–382.

Scott, V. (1989). An empirical study of explicit and implicit teaching strategies in foreign language teaching. *Modern Language Teaching, 73,* 14–22.

Scott, V. (1990). Explicit and implicit grammar teaching strategies: New empirical data. *French Review, 63,* 779–789.

Seow, A. (2002). The writing process and process writing. In J. C. Richards & W. Renandya (Eds.), *Methodology in language teaching: An anthology of current practice* (pp. 315–320). New York: Cambridge University Press.

Shaffer, C. (1989). A comparison of inductive and deductive approaches to teaching foreign languages. *Modern Language Journal, 73,* 395–403.

Shrum, J. L., & Glisan, E. (1994). *Teacher's handbook: Contextual language instruction.* Boston: Heinle & Heinle.

Shumin, K. (2002). Factors to consider: Developing adult students' speaking abilities. In J. C. Richards & W. A. Renandya (Eds.), *Methodology in language teaching: An anthology of current practice* (pp. 204–211). New York: Cambridge University Press.

Slavin, R. E. (1995). *Cooperative learning: Theory, research, and practice* (2nd ed.). Boston: Allyn & Bacon.

Stanovich, K. E. (1980). Towards an interactive-compensatory model of individual differences in the development of reading fluency. *Reading Research Quarterly, 16,* 32–71.

Tyler, R. (1949). *Basic principles of curriculum and instruction.* Chicago: University of Chicago Press.

Ur, P. (1996). *A course in language teaching: Practice and theory.* Cambridge, UK: Cambridge University Press.

Varah, L. J., Theune, W. S., & Parker, L. (1986). Beginning teachers: Sink or swim? *Journal of Teacher Education, 37,* 30–33.

Veenman, S. (1984). Perceived problems of beginning teachers. *Review of Educational Research, 54,* 143–178.

Williams, A., Prestage, S., & Bedward, J. (2001). Individualism to collaboration: The significance of teacher culture to the induction of newly qualified teachers. *Journal of Education for Teaching, 27*(3), 253–267.

Willis, D. (1986). The place of grammar in ELT. *TELL, 2*(2), 1–2.

Index

**CORWIN
PRESS**

The Corwin Press logo—a raven striding across an open book—represents the union of courage and learning. Corwin Press is committed to improving education for all learners by publishing books and other professional development resources for those serving the field of PreK–12 education. By providing practical, hands-on materials, Corwin Press continues to carry out the promise of its motto: **"Helping Educators Do Their Work Better."**